Make Sh** Happen

Defrag Your Mind

Deborah LeBlanc, CCHt, CAHA

Copyright © 2024 Deborah LeBlanc, CCHt, CAHA

All rights reserved.

The contents of this book may not be reproduced, duplicated, or transmitted without direct written permission from the author.

Under no circumstances will any legal responsibility or blame be held against the publisher for any reparation, damages, or monetary loss due to the information herein, either directly or indirectly.

Legal Notice:

This book is copyright-protected. This is only for personal use. You cannot amend, distribute, sell, use, quote, or paraphrase any part of the content within this book without the consent of the author.

Disclaimer Notice:

Please note the information contained within this document is for educational and entertainment

purposes only. Every attempt has been made to provide accurate, up-to-date, reliable, and complete information. No warranties of any kind are expressed or implied. Readers acknowledge that the author is not engaging in the rendering of legal, financial, medical, or professional advice. The content of this book has been derived from various sources. Please consult a licensed professional before attempting any techniques outlined in this book.

By reading this document, the reader agrees that under no circumstances is the author responsible for any losses, direct or indirect, which are incurred as a result of the use of the information contained within this document, including, but not limited to, errors, omissions, or inaccuracies.

Contents

	Introduction	5
1	**Find Your Focus**	**8**
	Meditation	8
	Hypnotherapy	9
	Yoga	10
	Listening to Music	10
	Breath Work	11
	Coloring or Drawing	13
	Journaling	13
	Tai Chi	14
	Acupuncture	14
	EFT Tapping	14
	Technology Cleanse	17
	Declutter Your Physical Space	17
	Other Mental and Physical Practices for Mindfulness	30
2	**Decide What You Want**	**33**
	Knowing vs. Hoping	34
	An Individual Practice	35
	Gratitude	36
	Boundaries	36

3	**Ignore the Rest**	**40**
	Ways to Unload Your Suitcase	45
4	**Cleaning Out the Recycle Bin**	**48**
	Freeing Up Your Mind	49
	To-Do Lists and Schedules	56
5	**Managing Habits**	**57**
	Eight Habits that Destroy Your Creativity	58
	How to Tell When a Habit is Bad	60
	Breaking Bad Habits	61
6	**Seek Novelty**	**67**
	How to Be a Novelty-Seeker	68
	Things to Do at Home with Kids	69
	Stay-at-Home Activities to Do with Friends	73
	Establishing a New Hobby	75
7	**Manage Your Mood**	**82**
8	**Get Your Sh** Together**	**118**
	Your Action Plan	121
Conclusion		**127**
Additional Resources		**129**
	Books	129
	Websites	140
	Podcasts featuring Deborah LeBlanc	142
	Other Podcasts	143
About the Author		**144**

Introduction

Welcome to Make Sh** Happen: Defrag Your Mind. What does it mean to defrag your mind, you might ask?

Defrag is short for *defragment*. In a computer, defragging rearranges the data on the hard disk. Data that is spread out all over the place gets nicely lined up. This results in more efficient storage. The computer can find what it needs faster, so it's more productive.

We're using that term in a general way to think about tidying up your mind (and your whole life) so that you are more productive and have more headspace for the things you love and want.

It may be helpful to think of your mind as a hard drive that needs to be cleared to make way for more current files.

The benefits of defragging your mind include boosting cognitive function, reducing stress and anxiety, enhancing creativity, and improving productivity.

We'll start our journey by exploring the many ways you can find mental clarity, like meditation, yoga, artwork, or acupuncture. Hopefully, you'll find two or three that you'd like to try. We'll also look at how important it is to declutter your physical environment.

In Chapter 2, we'll get very clear about what you want: your goals and priorities.

Next, in Chapter 3 we'll consider the baggage you're carrying around that forms obstacles to those goals and priorities.

Once you've identified those computer files in your brain that you no longer need, Chapter 4 identifies some techniques to let them go: ways to free up your mind for the life you choose.

So much of our life is determined by our habits that they deserve a chapter all their own. Chapter 5 takes a look at your habits and habitual patterns of thought and defrags them.

Chapter 6 switches to uploading the positive. It talks about how to see novelty and how enlivening new and unusual things are in our lives.

Like habits, moods can run our lives from the background without us even noticing. Chapter 7 explores five mood-management tools—physical activity, rewarding yourself, proper diet and nutrition, positive social interactions, and therapy—that are important to everyone.

Finally, we include a summary, some encouragement, and loads of resources so you can continue feeding your now-tidy mind. **Also included in Chapter 8 is a worksheet you can use as you read the book to create an inspiring action plan**.

So, what do you say? How about we start working to defrag your mind and improve your life? Let's do this!!

This is your time, your life, and your book.

"Clutter is not just physical stuff. It's old ideas, toxic relationships, and bad habits. It's anything that does not support your better self."

–Eleanor Brown

"If your mind isn't clouded by unnecessary things, then this is the best season of your life."

–Wu-men

"Open the window of your mind. Allow the fresh air, new lights, and new truths to enter."

–Amit Ray

"The greatest freedom is to be free of your own mind."

–Osho

Chapter One

Find Your Focus

> "If you take care of your mind, you take care of the world."
>
> –Arianna Huffington

There are many ways in which you can clear and center your mind, including meditation, hypnotherapy, yoga, listening to music, breathwork, coloring or drawing, journaling, tai chi, and EFT tapping.

Whatever activities make you feel calm and at peace can help you focus. Let's take a brief look at 12 common practices that increase focus so you can choose two or three to explore more deeply.

Meditation

Meditation is a practice in which a person exercises mindfulness—either guided, silent, or to music or binaural beats (two tones with slightly different frequencies at the same time). The purpose of meditation is to train your brain to be attentive and aware while achieving a calm and stable state of mind.

Hypnotherapy

Hypnotherapy, AKA hypnotic medicine or hypnotic suggestion, is not the stage acts you may have seen where a performer makes a line of volunteers act like monkeys at the snap of a finger. Instead, it is a therapeutic practice that uses hypnosis to help a client reach trance-like concentration and a heightened sense of suggestibility.

The goal is never for the person being treated with hypnotherapy to lose control over their bodies and minds. The aim is to allow them to access their subconscious mind while focusing and obtaining a goal that they desire—such as quitting a bad habit, attracting more money into their lives, healing from an injury or sickness, etc.

Hypnotherapy has been recognized by the American Psychological Association and American Medical Association as a valid procedure since the 1950s.

Due to the confusion over what hypnosis is and what it isn't, here are a few facts from a licensed hypnotherapist.

- Hypnotherapy is an altered state of consciousness like meditation, in which we help you connect with your subconscious mind.

- It is a natural experience that happens to most of us each day when we become absorbed in something like driving, daydreaming, reading, rhythmic exercises, or watching a favorite television program.

- It is about opening a small doorway in the critical mind, allowing you to bypass the conscious mind and access information in the subconscious. Once there, we help you uncover any limiting beliefs that were planted deep within years earlier and are now keeping you from reaching your full potential. You have the opportunity now to turn them into positives.

- You are fully aware of all of your senses while under hypnosis.

- Under hypnosis, our subconscious mind is usually very willing to respond to questions and help us resolve habits and issues that no longer serve us.

- It does not involve mind control, magic, or unconsciousness.

- You cannot be made to enter hypnosis against your will.

Yoga

Yoga is a group of physical, mental, and spiritual practices that originated in ancient India. The goal is to control or still the mind as you stretch and strengthen the body. You can find classes around your city or access online classes via YouTube and other sites in your home. The only thing to note as you get started is to take it slow. You don't want to do too much too quickly because you risk injury.

Listening to Music

For some, setting aside five minutes or more to pop in your headphones and listen to music you know will relax you is the key to mindfulness. This practice has been associated with helping people who suffer from anxiety, depression, ADHD, and more. It aids in bringing a person into the present. It can be used in conjunction with or in addition to meditation, hypnotherapy, and yoga.

Breath Work

Breath work helps you release toxins and stress as you breath out, and nourish your mind and body when you breath in. It has been found to help in the following areas:

- Balancing blood pressure
- Alkalizing your blood PH
- Improving time spent in deep sleep
- Reducing PTSD traumas
- Increasing respiratory functions
- Improving immune systems
- Releasing stress hormones
- Elevating your mood
- Decreasing addictive behaviors
- Improving mental focus

There are many different kinds of breath work techniques.

Deep Abdominal Breathing

This technique uses long, deep breaths. As you inhale, you picture your body filling up with air. Then, as you exhale, feel your chest relax and your belly pull back. This exercise is a way for you to tell your body to calm down. It can be used at any time—right before you give a big speech, get an injection, have to drive on the highway, or anything else that makes you feel anxious.

4-7-8 Breath

This is similar to deep abdominal breathing, but it adds counting beats into the mix. So you breathe in for four beats, hold for seven beats, breathe out for eight beats, and repeat. The longer exhale encourages you to completely empty your lungs.

Alternate Nostril Breathing

Start with your right thumb applying pressure to your right nostril. Then, inhale with only your left nostril and hold the breath while you switch sides, placing your right pointer finger to apply pressure to the left nostril. Then breath through that side only. This type of breathwork encourages balance in body and mind.

Breath of Fire

Considered to be a more advanced breath technique, this one requires you to relax your abdominal muscles while inhaling and then engage your core when exhaling forcefully to push air out of your body. It might take a few practices to get this right, but once you do, you will likely feel a sense of steadiness.

Holotropic Breathwork

It's best to work with an experienced instructor when learning this technique. However, the idea is to achieve a continuous inhale and exhale pattern with no pausing in between. This type of breathing floods your body with oxygen and renews your cells.

However, you should also know about the potential cons, including:

- Dizziness

- Tingling in your hands, arms, feet, and/or legs

- An irregular heartbeat

- Muscle spasms

- Changes in vision from lack of oxygen

- Ringing in your ears

If you experience any of the sensations above or other negative effects, you should stop your breathwork immediately and consult with your doctor.

Coloring or Drawing

There are plenty of adult coloring books available for purchase that might make you feel more at ease and content. Just drawing or any other type of art that might help you feel relaxed too.

Journaling

Daily journaling can help you reflect on your day and your mood throughout it. You can always go back and read old entries to examine patterns in your behavior. Moreover, a journal is a great place to air grievances about people or places without risking an actual confrontation. For instance, if you're mad at a coworker for talking over you in a meeting and you don't think it would be effective to discuss it, you can write them an uncensored letter in your journal. This will help you get all of your feelings out without risking a relationship.

Tai Chi

Often referred to as "meditation in motion," tai chi, which originated in China as a martial art, involves slow-motion exercises that move through a series of motions named after animal actions (like "white crane spreads its wings," for example) or martial arts moves (such as "box both ears") while breathing and without pausing.

This type of exercise helps focus your attention while promoting strength in your body. It is said to be one of the best techniques for people suffering from Parkinson's and other disorders affecting the nervous system, but it can improve the mind and body of anyone.

Like yoga, you can find tai chi classes around your city or look up online tutorials.

Acupuncture

This therapy also originated in China, and it involves the insertion of very thin needles through your skin at strategic points in your body to treat pain and achieve wellness and stress management.

Unlike other techniques we've talked about, you should not seek out this kind of treatment without the care of a professional.

EFT Tapping

Emotional Freedom Technique (EFT), AKA tapping or psychological acupressure, is an alternative or additive treatment for physical pain and emotional distress. Similar to acupuncture, EFT focuses on the energy hot spots in your body (although EFT only focuses on nine of the major ones) to balance your energy. There are no needles involved in EFT. Instead, you just use your fingers.

EFT can be divided into five steps.

1. **Identify the issue.** For the technique to be effective, you must first identify what issue or fear you are facing and hope to work on. This will influence the focal point of your tapping. Focusing on one problem at a time will enhance your desirable outcome.

2. **Test the initial intensity.** Once the target area is identified, you must next set a benchmark of intensity from zero to ten, with ten being the worst and most difficult emotional and physical pain you feel from the focal issue. This scaling helps you monitor your success after completing each EFT tapping session. For instance, if you started at a ten but ended at a five, you've achieved a fifty percent improvement level.

3. **The setup.** Once you've identified the issue and given it an intensity rating, you establish a phrase that explains what you're working on by focusing on the two main goals: acknowledging the issues and accepting yourself despite the problem. For example, a common setup phrase is: "Even though I have this [insert your fear or problem], I deeply and completely accept myself." However, be sure to address your problem instead of someone else's—i.e., don't say, "Even though my mom is sick..." Instead, say something like, "Even though I feel sad that my mom is sick..."

4. **EFT tapping sequence**. Although there are twelve major meridians that mirror each side of the body and correspond to an internal organ, EFT focuses on the following nine.
   - Side of hand, referred to as "karate chop" (KC): small intestine meridian
   - Top of head (TH): governing vessel
   - Eyebrow (EB): bladder meridian
   - Side of the eye (SE): Gallbladder meridian
   - Under the eye (UE): stomach meridian
   - Under the nose (UN): governing vessel
   - Chin (Ch): central vessel
   - Beginning of the collarbone (CB): kidney meridian
   - Under the arm (UA) spleen meridian

Begin by starting with the side of the hand point while reciting your phrase from above three times. Then, tap each ascending point seven times, moving down the body in this order: eyebrow, side of the eye, under the nose, chin, beginning of the collarbone, and under the arm. Finish by tapping the top of your head. Moreover, as you go through each ascending point, you should recite a reminder phrase—if your phrase is the example about your mother being sick, your reminder could be something like, "The sadness I feel that my mother is sick."

Repeat this entire sequence two to three times.

5. **Test the final intensity.** At the end of each sequence, rate your intensity from zero to ten. If you haven't reached zero, you may continue this process until you do.

Technology Cleanse

If you find that your mind is frantic, unfocused, or in another negative place, consider participating in a cleanse or detox from technology. This involves limiting or eliminating (if safe and possible given your job requirements) the amount of time you spend on your phone, tablets, and computers.

This time away from social media, world news, and other mentally draining words and imagery can bring clarity, self-confidence, and a better understanding of who you are. It may also help you develop deeper and better interpersonal relationships with the people around you. You might miss out on the latest celebrity death, major movie trailer, or other significant moment in history or pop culture, but it'll be worth it in the long run.

Declutter Your Physical Space

Decluttering your space—your home, office, or both—can help you gain focus, purpose, energy, and physical health. Many people find cluttered spaces to be distracting and overwhelming while cleaner ones promote productivity and mood.

If you want a deeper dive into this topic, check out my book *Make Sh** Happen: Unclutter Your Life.*

Tips for Decluttering

Here are a few tips from the above-referenced book (please feel free to skip this section if you've already read that book).

1. **Decide What You Want to Declutter**

When doing this, try to focus on specific locations instead of entire rooms. If you decide to start in the kitchen, don't simply focus on the kitchen as a whole. Instead, narrow it down to smaller areas, like pantry, cupboards, fridge, etc.

(Pro tip: It can be helpful to photograph entire rooms to determine which areas need the most urgent attention. And it will serve as a satisfying "before and after" once the room is organized to your liking.)

2. Plan Your Day

This is in a similar vein as the first point, but once you decide the areas in a room you want to tackle, plan your day (or weekend) in extreme detail, including setting times in which you should be done with each task. This will help you stay accountable and motivated. Don't forget to pencil in little breaks for coffee, stress walks around the block, or anything else you might need to keep chugging along with your cleaning.

(Pro tip: Starting the day with something small that will give you a "quick win" can help you gain momentum.)

3. Sort Items Into Three Piles

Organizing will likely feel less stressful and more effective if you have a clear and designated spot to put things. For example, piling junk on top of the things you want to donate or keep won't help anyone. So, when you decide what to organize, establish three piles: keep, donate/sell, and discard.

4. Choose What to Pass On

For some people, this can be hard, especially when an item that is taking up valuable space was gifted to you by a loved one or has other sentimental value to you. But the good news is 1) you don't have to tell people where gifts they've given you go, and 2) you don't have to get rid of everything. Regarding the second point, you can create a little box labeled "Memories" to keep special items, like your garter from prom, tickets from when you saw your favorite band for the first time, love notes, pictures, etc., in.

(Pro tip: Aside from the things that may not have much function in your life but still have special meaning, anything else should be assessed on their level of necessity in your life. Say you have a whole shelf of candles that are taking the space of something else, like precious photo albums filled with pictures of your children throughout the years. In that case, the candles can probably go.)

5. Decide What to Keep

As with the memory box we just mentioned, organizing isn't just about tossing or getting rid of the things you no longer need. On the contrary, it's also aimed at showing you things you may have forgotten about that are useful, bring you happiness, and/or spark the joy of old memories. For example, while cleaning your closet, you find a goofy old sweater that you and your friends wore for a dance during a high school assembly. You might want to keep that, perhaps in tandem with a photograph, to show your children someday how silly you were in your youth. Again, that is why this process is so highly specific to you. To some, such an item might instantly be thrown away or donated. But to others, it is really symbolic and something worth keeping.

6. Get Rid of Items Quickly

Once you've decided what to get rid of, throw them away, drop them off at a recycling or donation center, or put them online for sale as soon as possible. Holding onto them for prolonged periods of time doesn't help you get more organized. Instead, you'll just have bags of stuff around your house. Furthermore, the longer the items stay in your home, the more likely they are to be reintegrated back into your now-tidied drawers and closets.

Pro tip: If you are looking to donate clothes, please take extra care to make sure that the organization you're donating to is either non-profit (meaning the items will likely go to people in need) or for-profit (the funds from selling them will benefit others, such as the National Cancer Center, which has donation boxes that state the proceeds go toward the researching for a cure.)

7. Utilize Storage Solutions

There are plenty of attractive decorative boxes, stackable drawers, and other items that make storage—especially seasonal decorations or clothing, extra sheets and towels for visitors, etc.—easier and more appealing to the eye.

8. Develop a System

Labeling bins or folders can help you easily relocate and remember what things are inside. For example, old tax documents or Christmas decorations that you need or want to keep can be placed into one designated place, labeled, and then found when needed.

9. Celebrate Your Wins

As touched upon earlier, it's great to acknowledge and celebrate every success (no matter how small) when organizing your space. Pause after every successful day and reflect on all of the good that you did for yourself.

Different Types of Clutter (And How to Eliminate Them)

Please also be aware that there is more than one type of clutter. We won't touch on mental clutter here because it's touched on in other areas of this book, but here are two sources of noise in your life to consider.

"Noise" Clutter

This "noise" can be hard to wrap your mind around, but we'll do our best to help. Think of the things in your life that drive you crazy—like the fact that you can't seem to make it to work on time, you have a hard time saying no to plans you don't want to participate in, or you don't hit your workout goals for the week. Anything you set as a goal but don't accomplish can result in detrimental internal dialogue and/or the external criticism of others.

Neither outcome is desirable, so sticking to your goals and ambitions is a great way to alleviate this kind of "noise."

Further, having too many things going on at once can cause a kind of buzzing or other sound to appear in your head. That's the result of stress and being overwhelmed. If you find yourself in this position, talk to someone about how your load can be lightened at home or work. You can also make a list of things and cross them off one by one instead of looking at everything you have to get done.

Actual Noise

If you are like most people, you've lived in a duplex, dorm, or apartment sometime in your life. And if you have, you've also likely encountered a neighbor who plays music too loudly, hosts loud parties, has a heavy tread, or otherwise just produces a sound that irritates you. This is actual noise clutter.

If you feel comfortable addressing the issue personally, you should do so. But if not, that's what resident assistants and landlords are for.

You can encounter similar situations in other aspects of your life—at work, at the gym, etc. If it's a situation you can handle by speaking with the person responsible for producing the loud sounds, that's great. But if not—like if the music in a gym is too loud for your liking but the other patrons seem to have no issue with it—maybe it's time to find another place to work out or invest in some sound-canceling headphones if they are allowed in that establishment.

If you have sensitive hearing or get upset by loud noises, you may consider avoiding places like concerts, fairs, trampoline parks, or anywhere else where noise is inevitable. However, if you find that your sensitivities are ruining the overall quality of your life, you should consider speaking to your doctor or a therapist to address underlying issues and get help going forward.

Digital Clutter

Digital clutter can also come in two forms.

- Having too many screens in your life (constant attention on laptops, televisions, smartphones, etc.).

- Having disorganized filing on your laptop, desktop, phone, or tablet and having bloated email inboxes.

Too Many Screens

Whether at work or play, and whether it's our phones, computers, TVs, or tablets, it seems we're always looking at a flat surface that projects or reflects light.

Unfortunately, if your job requires you to look at a computer screen for long hours at a time, there isn't a whole lot you can do in terms of eliminating your screen time. However, you can get special glasses or activate your computer's settings to make the blue light less harmful to your eyes. Moreover, you can get special chairs or learn posture positions so that sitting for long periods of time does not put undue pressure on your neck, hips, and back.

If you have to endure extended screen time for your profession, you may want to consider trying to stay away from it at home. Reading a good book, drawing, playing with your pets, going for a walk, or cooking a meal are great alternatives to reading the news, scrolling social media, or binge-watching a show.

Here are a few harmful effects of too much screentime.

- Damage to your eyesight
- Interruptions in your sleep patterns
- Increased risk for obesity
- Poor posture (which can come with pain)
- Poor social skills
- Headaches
- Decreased attention

- Declines in mental health
- Poor core strength
- Decline in brain development for children

Disorganized Filing

Having endless unread emails, scattered desktop icons, and countless independent files are all examples of a disorganized computer. Such clutter inhibits your efficiency at work because you have to spend more time than a well-organized person would to locate something.

Here are a few tips for getting your digital files and folders tidied up.

Establish a clear hierarchy for your folder structure. This depends on the type of work you do. For example's sake, let's presume that you are a residential architect. In that case, your top-level folders may be "Bathroom Remodels," "Kitchen Makeovers," etc. Within those will be multiple folders and files pertaining to specific clients—"P. Johnson," "F. Smith," and "K. Williams."

Use a consistent naming convention for your files. In a similar vein, create naming conventions that will make it easy for you to locate certain documents. You can use keywords, pascal case, dates, version numbers, etc.

- **Keywords:** Including specific words like "invoice," "contract," etc., in your files makes them easier to retrieve *and* it makes it clear to your client what you're sending to them via email.
- **Use Pascal case:** If you're using compound words, capitalizing each first letter can make it easier to read. For example, "Johnson_AmendedAgreement" vs. "Johnson_Amendedagreement."

- **Add a date:** Starting each file with the date (e.g., yyyy.mm.dd or yy.mm.dd) of the correspondence, signatures, or whatever will automatically list them in chronological order in your folder.

- **Include the version number:** This is as simple as adding "v1," "v2," "v3," etc., to multiple iterations of the same document to locate the most recent (and likely current) version.

- **Sequential numbers:** If you want to arrange your files or folders in a particular order, adding a leading zero before each number (e.g., 01, 02, 03) will help you accomplish that.

- **Add "AA":** Another hack for organizing your files is by adding "AA" to the one you want at the very top. This will make finding your most important or most-used file easy to locate time and time again.

Add Tags

Suppose you are a cake decorator and you take pictures of your most impressive work to post on social media. You can add tags in addition to folder and filing structures. For example, you could add tags like "Birthday Cakes," "Wedding Cakes," etc., to quickly pull up examples for a prospective client.

Delete or Archive Unnecessary Files

At the end of every week or month, designate some time to go through folders and delete, rehome, or otherwise archive files you no longer need.

Keep Your Email Under Control

- Set up filters to funnel certain emails to different folders.

- Unsubscribe to spam.
- Clear out your inbox.
- Consider setting up two addresses: one for the things you want to be subscribed to, and another that you only give to friends and family.

Mental Clutter

Your mind becomes congested and unorganized when it is churning out too many thoughts—especially when they are unwanted, such as excuses not to do something that will only improve your life or harsh self-criticism. Mental clutter can also occur when you are juggling too many tasks at once.

A great way to eliminate mental clutter is by journaling to get your thoughts outside of your body and onto paper; meditating; going for a walk; making to-do lists; reducing the number of decisions you have to make; limiting screen time; setting priorities; and any other coping method you find useful in finding peace during the day.

Other Classifications of Clutter

There are other ways in which people categorize clutter.

- **Homeless clutter.** This is clutter in your home that doesn't have a designated spot. Later on, you're going to learn what we mean by "treating everything like a fork," and its purpose is to avoid this in your house.

    What to Do: Find a designated space for each item that you own. But if you can't, perhaps it's time to consider getting rid of the overflow items.

- **Fantasy or aspirational clutter.** These are things like weights, yoga mats, roller skates, or anything else that the ideal version of yourself would have *and* use. However, if you don't actually use them, they have no business being in your home. Clothes that don't fit you anymore or no longer align with your lifestyle and unused art/hobby supplies fall into this category.

  What to Do: Be honest and real with yourself. Say it's clothes that are too small for you. Are you going (and are you physically able) to take the steps to lose the extra weight to fit into them? If yes, you have to start now. If no, it might be time to part with them. However, this is certainly not a self-hate exercise. Let the shirt or pair of pants go with love. Your body, which is the vessel that allows you to be part of this world, once loved and looked good in them, but that isn't the case anymore. Maybe you had a baby, started taking a certain medication, suffered an injury and haven't been able to work out as often, etc. Whatever the case may be, if you're happy and healthy in your body, that's all that's important. Or maybe it's a pottery wheel that is taking up space in your garage. Ask yourself, "Am I really going to dedicate the time to learning how to use it?" If yes, start now. If no, find another home where it will be cherished and used.

- **Guilty, gifted, and inherited clutter.** Do you hold onto things like the nonsensical Mother's Day artwork that your children made you five years ago or that old clock that your father-in-law gave you but you've always hated? Those are examples of things we hold on to because we feel like we have to. But the truth is that you don't. You probably want to keep some childhood doodles and cards, and if that clock was dear to your partner's father or holds significance for him or her, you might consider holding onto it. But for anything you're comfortable with pitching, you should.

What to Do: Nobody wants to disrespect family members by throwing out heirlooms and gifts we've received from them. One way to skirt around this is by asking around and seeing if someone else wants Grandma's doll collection or your mom's tea set that she bought when she was eighteen. If they say no, then discuss whether or not *anyone* in the family needs to keep the item(s). If yes, perhaps you can consider upcycling it into something you will use. For example, say your grandfather had a beloved pocket watch that he carried everywhere with him. You (or a professional) can easily turn the face, hands, and other parts to create jewelry like earrings, necklaces, bracelets, etc. That way, you'll always have a piece of your grandpa with you, and you can look at the jewelry with fondness and in memory of him when you wear it.

- **Identity clutter.** This is one of the hardest to recognize, and to do so, you have to have some self-awareness. This refers to things you hold onto simply because they feel like they're a part of you (or the person you used to be or want to be). It's different from fantasy clutter because it can be stuff that was useful and used at one time. A great example of this is stay-at-home mothers. Sometimes, after their children have grown into teenagers or adults, they have a hard time getting rid of little books, toys, or anything else their child held dear. That's because they still identify as the mother of young children. But the harsh reality is they aren't anymore. As you'll read several times in this book, keeping *some* mementos are fine. But it's best to limit yourself to one small box. Anything else quickly starts to resemble clutter.

What to Do: It's simple (the solution...not always the process). Keep the small number of things that hold sentimental value, and either gift, sell, donate, or toss the rest.

- **Lazy clutter.** If you're the kind of person who takes something out of a cabinet, drawer, closet, etc., and just leaves it out, you likely have lazy clutter around your house. That's not a judgment; it's just the truth. Lazy clutter is anything that has a home but is not currently in that designated spot. Taking the brief amount of time it takes to put things back after you're done using them will eliminate this issue and leave you with a less cluttered house.

What to Do: This one is also a bit of a no-brainer. Just try to be better about cleaning up after yourself.

- **Other people's clutter.** This is probably one of the most infuriating types of clutter—your friends', family members', or whoever else's junk was dumped on you for whatever reason.

What to Do: Never, ever get rid of someone else's belongings without their permission. But this does not mean you can't give them warnings. For instance, suppose your friend left their Beanie Baby collection at your house (yes, this is a very specific example, but roll with it). You are a minimalist and don't want that kind of clutter in your house. Once your friend fails to come to pick it up a few times, you tell him or her that if it isn't gone in, say, a month (make it long enough to be reasonable on both your ends), you're going to take it into your own hands. That way, if they still don't get the crap out of your house, you are justified in getting rid of it.

***

No matter what type of clutter you have in your home, if it's bothering you and you want to enjoy a more minimalistic, cleaner house, find a way for you to feel guilt-free (or close to) and happy about getting rid of it. You and your improved mental health will be glad you did.

Other Mental and Physical Practices for Mindfulness

These are things you can do to help you stay focused in the moment.

- **Avoid multitasking.** Do one task at a time until it is finished and only then move onto the next.

- **Work in blocks of time.** You have a unique attention span, and you can find out what it is by reading a book and noticing when your mind starts to drift from the words on the page. Once you discover how long your attention is at its peak, you'll be able to work in those time increments going forward, take a break when necessary, and then resume the activity.

- **Remove distractions.** While you're working on a task, remove potential distractions. They may include a television screen, phone, pet, or another person. The TV is probably the easiest thing to resist because you can just turn it off. It may be beneficial for you to put your phone in a drawer or another room so it won't tempt you from completing whatever work you have to do. Or you can block certain websites and calls for certain periods of time. For a pet, you don't want to neglect them, but if it's reasonable to part with them for the amount of time you need to concentrate, you can always close yourself in another room for a bit. Finally, if it's another person (spouse, roommate, etc.), hopefully, you can simply tell them that you need space, and they will respect that.

- **Take a quick exercise break.** Even just ten minutes of moderate-intensity running or walking increases the blood flow to the prefrontal cortex, which is the part of the brain that is responsible for executive functions, like staying focused.

These are lifestyle changes that you can implement to maintain a healthy brain.

- **Stay mentally engaged.** Just like the muscles in your body, your brain needs frequent exercise to achieve its peak performance. The good news is that there are plenty of ways in which you can work out your brain—doing a puzzle, taking a class, volunteering, or joining a book club.

- **Get enough rest.** Seven to nine hours of sleep per night can help you stay alert, focused, and energized. If you find it hard to fall or stay asleep, talk to your doctor about potential underlying health conditions, such as restless leg syndrome, sleep apnea, joint pain, etc., that may be causing an issue for you.

- **Check your medication.** Many prescription and over-the-counter medications can make you drowsy and/or less focused. If you feel tired throughout the day, talk with your pharmacist about the ingredients in medications and/or consult with your doctor about switching meds or lowering dosages.

- **Watch your caffeine intake.** While caffeine has been proven to increase attention, too much can cause you to be anxious and unfocused. The FDA considers 400 milligrams of caffeine, which is found in four to five cups of coffee, to be a "safe" daily intake for healthy adults. Experiment to find out how much gives you a mental jolt without feeling jittery.

We hope that you will take any number of these suggestions and implement them to defrag your mind while improving your emotional, mental, and physical well-being.

Chapter Two
Decide What You Want

> "When we clutter our lives with imagined obligations, unnecessary activities, and distractions that only kill time, we dilute the power of our lives."
>
> –Anne Katherine

When seeking mental clarity, it's important to identify the things that you want first. A great way to do this is by thinking about your long-term priorities. For example, let's say you want more financial stability in your life. Well, if that's the case, everything you do through meditation, hypnotherapy, and in daily thoughts can be directed toward that goal.

Whatever you project in life—be it money, health, etc.—you attract into your life. This also goes for negative things. For instance, it has been said that worrying is like praying for what you do *not* want to happen to occur. Think about that the next time you're stuck in a spiral of negative thoughts. It's not always the easiest process, but with practice, you'll likely find that you can turn a bad thought into a positive one.

However, just like deciphering what you want, you must first identify when you're stuck in a pattern of negativity. If you struggle with this, which is normal and understandable, here are a few prompts to get you on the right track.

Problem: Money

First indication	Recognize the thought	Next step	Change
Feeling negative about your financial situation (i.e., assessing how much money other people have in relation to what you lack, being afraid to look at your bank statements, etc.)	Catch yourself and take a second to fully come to terms with your relationship with money.	Recognize that these thoughts are keeping you from the fortune you desire.	Go forward with a more positive affirmation (like, "Money is everywhere," "Money falls easily into my life," and "I am a money magnet.")

Once you change your relationship with and thought patterns around money, you'll find it springing up everywhere in your life. Don't trust us? Try it for yourself!

The same goes for anything else in your life you wish you had—less anxiety, better health, happiness, a new group of friends, a romantic partner, anything!

Take a second to look around you. Everything you have (or don't have) in your life is in direct correlation to your mental attitude toward it.

Knowing vs. Hoping

Even given all of that, however, is the caveat that you must genuinely *know* the positive statements you're thinking about. This means you can't think, "Ooh, I *hope* I attract more money into my life." No. You must *know* your power and that you will. Hope indicates doubt—you're thinking there's a chance things will turn out how you want them to. In essence, you're wishing for something to happen.

One way to ensure that you're knowing instead of hoping is by thinking about whatever you want as something that's already yours. Suppose you have a bill due in a few days but you don't have the money to cover it. Well, start transforming your mind into thinking that you already have it, and you'll be able to pay it without any worry or problem. Again, don't *hope* this will come true. *Know it.* See the funds flooding into your bank account. Picture them over and over and over again.

If it helps, come up with little sayings about the money (or whatever else you want to attract into your life) that *is already yours.*

Furthermore, knowing is faith. Hoping is not.

Do you have faith that you're a strong enough being to manifest just about anything you want into your life? We *know* you can.

An Individual Practice

It's also important for you to understand that you can only attract things on behalf of yourself. As much as we may want to rid our family members, children, etc., of illness, depression, or sickness, the unfortunate truth is that we can't.

Instead, the best thing you can do is teach them about the mindfulness activities touched on in the first chapter and run through the process outlined above with them.

If they're receptive to all of this, they will start changing their lives for the better too.

Gratitude

Another key aspect of manifesting what you want is being grateful for the things that are already in your life. Let's stick with the money example. Perhaps you feel stuck in your small apartment but can't afford the house of your dreams.

Well, you know what won't attract the funds for that home? Feeling sorry for yourself. This is harsh, but it's an essential bit about manifestation that people miss.

Instead, take a moment, maybe when you get up in the morning or during another opportune time, and feel truly grateful for that small apartment. Think about how the ceiling and walls protect you from bad weather, cold and hot temperatures, and other people with bad intentions. Then, look at everything you have in that apartment—your bed that you sleep soundly on at night, the clean water that comes out of the faucets, an oven that you cook your meals on, a comfy couch where you and your friends watch your favorite shows together, etc.

Once you start thinking in gratitude, you'll start attracting more of what you want. Just remember that you don't manifest more based on thoughts and feelings of lack. Lack only favors more lack.

One more helpful hint about this: one of the most powerful mantras or positive affirmations you can have is, "I lack nothing." The more you think and feel this, the better off your life will be.

Boundaries

We've presented you with many ways of learning to focus, dealing with clutter, identifying what you most want, and manifesting it. Obviously, you could spend all day practicing techniques, but that's neither possible nor helpful.

On the contrary, overcommitting yourself to tasks, plans, and affirmations only clutters your mind. How to prioritize?

Tasks

Part of defragging your mind is prioritizing what needs to be done in terms of your work, chores, the care of your children, etc. But you aren't a superhero. You're a human being, just like the rest of us. So, at the start of every week or day, sit down and decipher what *needs* to be done.

Aside from the basics that come with being an adult, like paying bills, going to work, and caring for family, this list will be different for everybody.

When deciphering your "needs" list, please choose carefully. There's an aspect of integrity that comes with completing the tasks you set out to do. If you are continually making lists and disregarding them, you aren't staying true to your word, and you are likely doing that in other aspects of your life.

Plans

When it comes to plans, either with your friends, coworkers, or family, you should prioritize based on what you need to do and what you *want* to do.

Perhaps you've had a particularly hard week dealing with a sick child or a busy work schedule. Well, in that case, maybe you don't need to go to the dinner you scheduled with a friend before you know how difficult your life was going to be. If you feel like you could benefit from some rest, tell your friend that. If they care and value you, they'll understand.

However, you want to have a true, clear reason for canceling plans. Otherwise, you're making *bad* excuses. Moreover, if you find that you are rescheduling or canceling plans with the same people over and over again, you should probably take a minute to assess whether or not you actually like being around them. This is trickier for family members than casual friends but breaks from both (as long as they don't depend on you financially, physically, etc.) are okay—as long as you go about it with respect for all parties involved.

Values

It may seem funny for us to go on and on about the importance of positive affirmations and then tell you to limit them...but having too many won't get you anywhere either. Why? Because you have to be specific about the things you want.

Here's a list of values. Please pick out your top six (and don't think too hard about them...go with your gut) and write each one on a sticky note. Feel free to add any others that you can think of.

Wealth	Happiness	Self-awareness	Honesty	Forgiveness
Abundance	Love	Romance	Adaptability	Balance
Family	Honor	Health	Accountability	Harmony
Humor	Prosperity	Success	Courage	Freedom
Gratitude	Fun	Honor	Commitment	Loyalty
Security	Safety	Acceptance	Creativity	Confidence
Ambition	Friendship	Compassion	Honesty	Adventure
Leadership	Challenge	Beauty	Authority	Community
Authenticity	Curiosity	Fairness	Faith	Determination
Influence	Justice	Kindness	Optimism	Peace
Pleasure	Respect	Spirituality	Wisdom	Integrity

Once you have your six, lay each note out before you.

Then eliminate three so you are left with your top three values. These are your most important values (and they can change and swap out with others at any time). Try to focus on them as you develop and recite your affirmations.

Chapter Three

Ignore the Rest

> "Keeping baggage from the past will leave no room for happiness in the future."
>
> –Wayne L. Misner

It may be helpful to think of the stress you carry around as luggage: physical weight you carry around as you live your life. Not only you can feel it; it's likely that others around you can too.

So ask yourself, what is and what isn't necessary for you to be lugging around?

If you're unsure of whether you're carrying around emotional or mental baggage, here are a few signs to consider.

- Difficulty letting go of past experiences

    ◦ Examples: Being unable to forgive yourself and others for past mistakes, holding grudges or being unable to move forward due to past experiences, constantly bringing up past events, or being unable to stop bringing up an ex.

- Potential causes: Trauma that has not been processed.

- Potential effects: The hindrance of personal growth and prevention of living independently and in the present.

• Chronic stress and anxiety

- Examples: Constant worrying, social anxiety, feelings of impending doom, physical symptoms (such as headaches, stomach problems, and sleep disturbances), restlessness, and difficulty focusing.

- Potential causes: Emotional issues from the past that have not been sufficiently processed or dealt with. (This is not addressing brain chemistry and/or hormonal changes.)

- Potential effects: Various physical health issues (which, according to the National Institutes of Health, may include arthritis, hypertension, asthma, stroke, chronic pain, heart disease, and peptic ulcers).

• Difficulty forming healthy relationships

- Examples: Repeatedly getting involved in toxic or unhealthy relationships, being unable or unwilling to fully commit to positive relationships, and the inability to set healthy boundaries and/or communicate effectively.

- Potential causes: Trauma.

- Potential effects: A pattern of toxic relationships, trust issues, and commitment problems.

- Negative self-image

  - Examples: Constant self-criticism, low self-esteem, feeling unworthy of love and happiness, and comparing oneself negatively to others.

  - Potential causes: Past rejection, failure, or criticism.

  - Potential effects: Being held back in almost every area of life (work, home, romantic, etc.)

- Avoidance of emotional intimacy

  - Examples: Avoiding deep conversations or one's feelings, being uncomfortable with vulnerability, and keeping others at a distance to avoid being hurt by them.

  - Potential causes: A defense mechanism to protect oneself from others.

  - Potential effects: The prevention of developing deep connections with other people.

- Frequent mood swings

  - Examples: Being overly sensitive or having sudden and unexplained changes in mood, experiencing intense emotional reactions to minor events, and having difficulty controlling emotions, leading to outbursts or withdrawal.

  - Potential causes: Unresolved emotional issues that have not been processed. (This is not addressing brain chemistry and/or hormonal changes.)

- Potential effects: Instability in relationships and daily life.

- Self-sabotaging behaviors

  - Examples: Procrastinating or self-destructive habits, constantly setting oneself up for failure, and rejecting opportunities for success or happiness.

  - Potential causes: A way to confirm one's negative self-beliefs about the ability to succeed and be loved and/or the fear of being rejected.

  - Potential effects: Missing out on all of the positive and wonderful things life has to offer (like success, happiness, and love).

- Hypervigilance and overreaction to triggers

  - Examples (which can be sudden or become a regular pattern): Exhaustion and emotional burnout due to the heightened state of alertness and perceiving threats when there aren't any.

  - Potential causes: Reminders of past trauma or negative experiences.

  - Potential effects: A diminished peace of mind and quality of life.

- Fear of abandonment or rejection

  - Examples: Constantly seeking reassurance and fearing the end of relationships.

- Potential causes: Being rejected by significant people (parent, spouse, etc.)
- Potential effects: Needy or clingy attachments to people or avoidance of new relationships and paranoia.

Aside from the emotions and thoughts above, you may also suffer from mental baggage if you experience the following consistently:

- Helplessness
- Loneliness
- Resentment
- Jealousy
- Anger
- Sadness
- Despair
- Hatred
- Overwhelm
- Feeling out of control
- Scared
- Hopeless
- A racing mind
- Fatigue

Ways to Unload Your Suitcase

However, the good news is that if you do suffer from any of the above mental and emotional baggage (and most, if not all, of us do), there are plenty of strategies to help you deal with them. (Several of these have already been introduced in the first two chapters, but they work for both mental clearing and healing as well.)

Strategy	**Why it works**	**Benefits**
Self-reflection and journaling	You're taking time out of your day to reflect on your feelings and experiences. Plus, you can write things down on a page that you may never dream of saying to another person. Moreover, you can reflect on older entries.	Increased self-awareness and understanding
Meditation and/or hypnotherapy	Both can make you more aware of your emotions and thoughts while aiming to foster a deeper understanding and acceptance of you and your past experiences.	Reduced stress and improved mental health

Support groups	Speaking with others who have gone through the same or similar things can give you a sense of community and a shared sense of understanding.	Peer support and shared understanding
Educational workshops and seminars	They focus on personal growth, emotional intelligence, and relationship skills.	Enhanced personal and relational skills
Physical activity	It can release emotions and stress that you've pent up.	Improved mental and physical health
Self-help books	Exploring books that provide insight and strategies for dealing with your mental and emotional baggage.	Self-guided learning and personal development
Life coaching or therapy	Work with professionals who have gone through similar things to develop social skills and learn strategies for overcoming personal challenges.	Goal-oriented personal development

| Online resources and communities | There are plenty of online platforms that you can access for resources to help you work through emotional baggage. | Accessible support and information |
| Creative expression | Engaging in arts and creative expression are great outlets for emotional and mental healing. | Emotional expression |

We hope you've learned to identify baggage you may be carrying around and gained some strategies to start jettisoning all of it out of your life for good.

And if you find that you are being weighed down, please do not feel ashamed or like something is wrong with you. Instead, see this as an opportunity for growth and personal development, two things that will only make you a more well-rounded, compassionate, and content human being.

Chapter Four

Cleaning Out the Recycle Bin

> "Nothing can bring you peace but yourself."
> –Ralph Waldo Emerson

As we've discussed, defragging your mind is similar to clearing files on your computer.

The goal for both is to identify and delete the files (or emotions, thoughts, and opinions) that are no longer useful or serving us. Then you have space to create more recent or positive ones in their place.

If the luggage or computer analogies didn't stick with you, try thinking of your mind as a mason jar of perishable food—let's say grapes. Picture it in your mind full to the brim with grapes. Now, especially if some of the grapes have gone bad (think of those negative thoughts or baggage), you need to fish them out and replace them with fresher ones. Those fresh grapes are the changes you need to make in your mind. Ditch the pruned, gross ones for some that are shiny and have a beautiful tone of red.

And don't be afraid to take those new grapes out and admire them! You did a good thing, after all, by replacing those that make you sick with some that are both nice to look at and healthy for you to consume.

In this chapter, we'll look at different ways to prune what no longer serves you, keep what does, and free up space for new, refreshing content.

Freeing Up Your Mind

One way to get your negative or unwanted thoughts, feelings, and emotions out of your physical body is by writing them down.

We already covered journaling in general. You can write long-form letters to yourself or to the journal as a person/friend you're divulging your secrets to. Or you can just "word vomit" anything you feel you would benefit from writing down on paper.

However you decide to go about it, journaling is a great way to express and heal yourself. Once you get everything out, you can preserve only the good, productive, and helpful stuff in your mind.

10 Steps for Emotive Journaling

Research has shown that accepting your mental experiences is linked with greater psychological health. Here's one way to work on acceptance.

- **Pick one memory.** Identify a memory that you want to reflect on and work from. Then, rate it on a scale from ten (very upset) to zero (not upset at all) based on how it makes you feel. Emotive journaling works best for memories that score between one to six (something that is mildly or moderately upsetting). While some people are better than others at processing stronger memories, most require the help of a professional (like a therapist) to work with them.

- **Get nice and comfy.** Pick a time and place where you know you won't be distracted. Reserve twenty to thirty minutes for mildly upsetting memories and up to ninety for moderately upsetting ones. Remember that you want enough time to get everything out, and you don't want to get interrupted. Choose a place where you feel safe and comfortable. You may also want to wear your most comfortable clothes, have your dog or cat right next to you, drink your favorite tea out of your go-to mug, or play your favorite music in the background. Whatever you can do to make yourself feel cozy is good to include in this process.

- **Vividly relive.** Next, and this is often the hardest part for people, allow yourself to relive the memory. See everything, hear every word or sound, and focus on how all of it made you feel. The facts are helpful, but it's really the feelings you want to capture. So try to use as many "feeling" words as you can—scared, excited, worried, sad, confused, etc.

- **Write or type your feelings.** Now that you've allowed yourself to relive and feel, you can either write or type everything down. Both methods are calming ways to draw your emotions out of your body and mind.

- **Take a comfy break.** Once you've gotten everything down, set your journal or laptop aside and focus on the comfort items you've collected around you. Drink your tea, pet your animals, savor the music, or eat a yummy snack for a minute or two.

- **Repeat, repeat, repeat.** Emotive journaling is like learning how to ride a bike in that you have to do it over and over again (hopefully improving each time) before you get the hang of it. It may be especially helpful to write about the same memory until you find that you're rating it a zero or one on the scale of how upset it makes you.

- **Consider a do-over.** Once you've processed the memory for what it was and it no longer upsets you as it did in the past, take some additional time to think and write (or type) about what you wish you would've done differently in the same scenario. For instance, think of what you could've done or said to make the situation better than it was.

- **Practice the new way.** Now that you've gone through the experience of analyzing your behavior, hopefully, you'll be able to present yourself differently to the world and better handle things in the future. If you find yourself getting upset by someone or something, think back to your do-over and implement some of those things.

Physical, Cognitive, and Emotional Benefits of Journaling

Although the act of journaling can be stress-inducing, in the long run, it's considered to have certain physical and cognitive benefits, including:

- Lower blood pressure

- Improved lung and fiver function

- Less time spent in the hospital

- Better moods

- Fewer sick days from work

- Higher academic grades
- Reduced stress-related doctor visits
- Fewer depressive and avoidance symptoms

Journal is effective because it involves the following processes.

- **Emotional catharsis.** There is an emotional release of unconscious conflicts through venting negative feelings.
- **Increased cognitive processing.** This is time spent creating coherent narratives of what has happened to you.
- **Repeated exposure.** Increased and prolonged exposure to stressful events may lead to a reduction in harmful thoughts and feelings.
- **Emotional inhibition.** Actively inhibiting negative emotions takes considerable effort, which further stresses the body and the mind. But by confronting them, you may be supporting cognitive integration and further understanding.

Additional Guidance

If you're just starting with journaling, or you want to get even deeper into it than you are now, here are some other things to consider before you start your first (or next) session.

- Pick the time of day that suits you best to sit down and write. Setting a regular time is helpful, but life happens, so please accept it when you have to be a little flexible.

- Start by expressing your feelings, allowing yourself to identify and name each one. Then move on to observing your thoughts and patterns of thinking you fall into.

- Start small. Being by writing only a few minutes. You may want to start every session by jotting down a few things that happened to you that day or something that has been troubling you. Once you're comfortable with that, it may help you open up to writing more deeply.

- Express what you want from life and how you feel about it. There are no rules for doing this, so don't hold back.

- Choose a medium that suits you. Some people write in paper journals or type on laptops. You can also record your spoken voice.

There are also journaling apps, like:

- ClickUp is a productivity platform designed to manage your schedule, goals, and more (free).

- The Five Minute Journal. Based on a successful hardcover journal, you'll get prompts every morning on your phone like "I am grateful for..." and "What will I do today to make it great?" Then, at night, you'll receive similar notifications like "Jot down three amazing things that happened to you today" and "How could I have made today better?" (one-time fee)

- Day One, a free-form, open-ended digital diary (annual subscription).

- Penzu – similar to Day One, a free-form diary app (annual subscription).

- Dabble.me – this one is similar to The Five Minute Journal app, but it sends prompts to your email. Rather than direct prompts, it open-endedly asks you how your day was or reminds you of answers you've provided in the past (annual subscription).

- Daybook – like Day One or Penzu because of its minimalistic design (free).

- Journey.cloud – the most popular app on this list and an up-to-date version of Day One, Penzu, and Daybook because, for example, you can create entries via email and social media posts into your entries (annual subscription).

- Daylio is a "micro diary and mood tracker" that is an alternative to traditional journaling apps (one-time fee).

- 750 Words. As the name suggests, this app suggests that you write 750 words each day in a stream of consciousness (annual subscription).

- GoodNotes. This one is best for visual thinkers because you can create shapes, add photos, use different highlighter colors, and write in your handwriting (one-time fee).

- Momento – a multi-purpose private journal to record your to-do lists, goals, and more (free for basic; premium version by subscription).

• Accept that you may feel upset as you write. That's okay and kind of the whole point. Take a break whenever you need to (the short-term distress is usually seen as nothing compared to the long-term benefit).

- If you have a hard time getting going, start with a prompt, like:

  - How have recent changes in your life made you feel? If you're struggling with them, have you always responded to change in this way? Can you think of any other examples?

  - What are you most anxious or uncertain about? Where is that coming from, and what are you doing to cope with those feelings? If you think you need to be doing more, in what ways can you receive and access help?

  - What are three things you are most grateful for today, or what three good things have happened to you today?

  - What are your favorite memories from your own or your children's lives?

  - What is something you fear? Why do you think this scares you? Has it always?

  - What do you enjoy doing, and why?

  - How would you describe yourself from the perspective of someone close to you? (Pick a family member, significant other, friend, child.)

  - What would your very best day look like, and why?

  - If you woke up tomorrow having everything you truly wanted, what would your life look like?

- Do you consider yourself a happy person? If not, or even if so, what could you do to make your life happier?

- Do you think your childhood self would be proud of the person you are now?

• Don't worry about spelling and punctuation. What's important are the words and nothing else.

• Remember that your journal is private, and make sure that your family members, partner, or roommates know that it is not for them to look at. They will only ever learn about an entry if you choose to tell them about it or read it out loud to them.

To-Do Lists and Schedules

Like journaling, it's also great to get your lists and schedules out of your mind and on paper. So having a physical paper calendar, a large dry-erase board in your house, using your Google calendar, or having another calendar app on your phone are all great ways to save some mental space.

Chapter Five

Managing Habits

> "Keep your head clear. It doesn't matter how bright the path is if your head is always cloudy."
>
> –Unknown.

Many of us like to think of ourselves as independent, free-willed people. However, that isn't necessarily the truth. Instead, we are creatures of habit. Why? Because it makes life easier.

Think about it. Without our habits or routines, we'd be paralyzed with endless deliberations throughout the day. It would start from the moment we woke up in the morning—do we shower, eat breakfast, feed the dog, and then get dressed? Or do we eat breakfast, feed the dog, shower, and then get dressed? And so on and so forth.

Habits are also comforting because they enable us to know what to expect in our daily lives. For example, you likely almost always take the same route to work because you know what the traffic patterns are usually like or how long the traffic lights are. If you walk for exercise, you probably take the same or similar route each time because you know what the terrain is like, how busy that path or sidewalk is, etc.

So habits have their uses. However, some habits are unhealthy, keep you from advancing in life, and hold your creativity back.

Eight Habits that Destroy Your Creativity

Learning to think creatively is a critical part of changing the world, but if you've been chugging along without much success, make sure you aren't engaging in these negative habits.

- **Assuming things will "just happen."** Many believe that the best bursts of creativity are spontaneous. But this spontaneity doesn't exist in isolation. More often than not, you have to schedule time to allow your creative process to happen. So, the more time you allow for it, the more creative you will become.

- **Failing to support the creative process.** You can't create something when you don't have the appropriate means to do so. For instance, if you want to write a book, in today's day and age, you can't do so without a working computer, a word processor, and the ability to type. Or let's say you want to create a painting. You can't do that without a canvas, paints, and the necessary brushes. Make sure you have the support and tools you need before working on an endeavor or goal. If you don't, you'll fail before you even start.

- **Ignoring the opinions of others**. This doesn't mean you should listen to the negative opinions of others who are just trying to drag you down. But creativity and innovation take a village. Listen with an open heart to the criticism of people who want to see you—and whatever you're creating—succeed. How to tell the difference between constructive vs. deconstructive criticism? Constructive criticism uplifts, offers helpful suggestions, and provides potential solutions. Deconstructive criticism mocks, points out flaws, and doesn't offer support or solutions.

- **Multitasking.** Only a small percentage of us on this earth are capable of true multitasking. The rest of us might try to do it, but we will more than likely fail. Our creativity diminishes as we struggle to focus on two or more things.

- **Insisting on perfectionism.** Your ideas don't have to be perfect to be effective. In fact, the best ideas often come out of many trials and failures. Remember, "good enough" is usually… good enough. Perfectionism can destroy your productivity and prevent you from accomplishing what you would've been able to if you accepted a lower standard of quality.

- **Getting stuck in the research phase.** Granted, information is important, and you can't start on a project without first having the base knowledge for it. However, too much information can overwhelm your mind and squelch the creative process.

- **Letting yourself get stuck in a rut.** If you feel stuck in the same routines you've had for as long as you can remember, don't be afraid to try new methods to accomplish the same thing. Highly creative people are always seeking out new experiences and new ways of doing things.

- **Believing that social time doesn't take you away from your creative time.** More often than not, the best creative ideas come when you're away from others and their ideas. We're not suggesting you become a hermit or anything. But giving yourself the time and grace to disengage from your peers and social media and to think and create is totally fine.

We focused on creativity in this list, but really the bullet points can be applied to any area in your life that you wish to change and defrag.

They can be applied to any thought process or opinion—be it about politics, science, general morals, relationships, etc.

More often than not, when we are intentional and focused and only allow positive criticism, don't overwhelm ourselves with too much information, take time for ourselves, and make sure we have adequate support, we come out on the other side with a better understanding of ourselves and the world around us.

However, there may be habits in your life that are holding you back, and you might not even recognize them as anything other than part of your normal routine.

We hope you're seeing now that certain "r" words—routine and rut—can be dangerous if you don't address or handle them appropriately.

However, before we dive more into this, it's important to note that what one person deems a bad habit isn't so bad for someone else. For example, say someone's body has a hard time processing dairy, and when he or she does, they become very sick. Well, to that person, a habit of going to get an ice cream cone at Dairy Queen every week could be considered bad, when the same action in someone who wasn't lactose intolerant could be perfectly healthy.

How to Tell When a Habit is Bad

In general, a bad habit fits the following criteria.

- It keeps you from being the best version of yourself (and sometimes only you can decide what that is).

- It harms your health or wellness (again, this can be different among individuals—but in general, smoking, excessive alcohol intake, doing illegal drugs, and things like that are pretty universally detrimental).

- Repetitive negative behavior patterns.

- You can stop the behavior with willpower and perseverance (unlike a medical condition, for example).

- It causes you to make bad excuses (again, "bad" excuses are not grounded in truth).

- It's illegal and could harm someone else and/or get you into trouble with the law.

- You rationalize and justify the behavior to yourself and others.

Breaking Bad Habits

The first and perhaps hardest step in breaking a bad habit is to recognize and admit that it exists.

After that, there are several conscious steps (meaning you have to actively decide to go against the habit) to identify, disrupt, and replace a bad habit.

Identify cues. Every habit has a trigger: something that cues it up. Suppose you had what you considered a bad habit of eating too much chocolate. Well, that habit could be triggered by a stressful situation, such as a big project at work or a breakup. Chocolate might bring you the comfort you reach for during those times. When cleaning up and getting organized, for another example, the second you walk into your kitchen and see a pile of dishes, you might feel overwhelmed and triggered to start making excuses as to why you shouldn't do them...you're too busy, you can always just do them tomorrow, you're a bad person (and a bad housekeeper) for not doing them, so there's no reason to even try, etc. Understanding your triggers is very important because they are what put your habits into motion.

Disrupt the triggers. Once you understand your triggers, you can throw them off kilter. One of the greatest examples of this is about your alarm clock. If you find that you struggle with getting up on time because you're constantly hitting the snooze button, a way to disrupt that habit is by putting your phone across the room. That way, you'll have to physically get up (which will disrupt the snooze habit) and turn the alarm off.

Replace the bad habit. Replacing a bad old habit with a new positive one is a great way to eliminate the behaviors in your life that do not serve you. Say you've noticed that there's a weird smell in the back of your car and you suspect the aroma is coming from the piling heaps of garbage you've discarded there. Each time you get in your car, you may feel triggered to think negatively about yourself. Well, a great habit to replace that with is just cleaning it up once and for all. Going forward, if a similar issue arises, you won't keep putting it off. Instead, you'll clean it immediately (or prevent it from ever getting to that state again). Being triggered to clean up a mess is much healthier than putting it off.

Keep it simple. Breaking the habit of making excuses and putting off cleaning or organizing the spaces you occupy should be done in small and simple steps. We're not suggesting that you need to make it a habit to vacuum out every nook and cranny of your vehicle once a day. Instead, you should try to disrupt and replace your old habits of letting junk pile up on the floor. An example of a smaller step would be committing to get a little garbage can that you empty once a week. This will be much more successful than any large change you try to make.

Think long-term. Whenever you're struggling with abandoning a bad habit, it's best to think in the big picture. When you encounter the need to take out the trash, consider why you want to do that instead of keeping it inside your house. It may be because your long-term goal is to have a clean and tidy house to raise your family in. If that's the case, continually picture what your dream house will look like. Every day, you're making decisions and efforts, like taking the trash out when it's full, to get closer to that vision. Once you reach that goal, you'll have to continue working toward keeping your house that way.

Persist. What's great about our brains is that positive behaviors, when done over and over again, become positive habits. So, keep at them!

Because this book specifically is about defragging our minds, here are a few examples of changing a negative mental habit into a positive one.

Habit	Identifying the Trigger	Disrupting the Bad Habit	Replacing the Habit and Persisting with a New, Simple One
Telling yourself you're not enough.	When do you notice telling yourself this most often? Is it when you look at yourself in the mirror? When you get dressed in the morning?	Once you've established the trigger, you'll know when you're most apt to think negatively about yourself. Then, instead, think something like, "Wow, I'm really beautiful." Repeat that affirmation over and over again throughout the day.	If you stay consistent with that affirmation, you'll soon find that it is what comes to mind when you encounter that trigger. And you've turned a bad habit into a positive one!

Feeling badly about your money situation. (Feeling and telling yourself that you're broke).	When do you feel or think like this? Is it when you're at the store? When you're paying your bills? Or maybe when you are about to log into your account?	Recognize when you're feeling or thinking about being broke. Then stop, change your attitude, and think something like, "I lack for nothing," "I am abundant," or "Money flows easily to me."	As long as you remain persistent in changing the way you think and feel about money, you'll find that your financial situation will change and improve.
When you sit down to accomplish a task, your mind floods with all the other things you have to get done that day.	When does this happen? If you need to get work done, it might be when you sit down at your computer. If you need to clean, it may be when you grab a broom or rag.	Purposefully focus your mind on the task at hand.	Focus on the specific goal or task you want to complete. Say you need to fill out an expense report. Well, anything else on your checklist should be put on the back burner while you devote all focus to completing that report. The other things can wait. Plus, with increased attention, you're likely to get the report done right the first time (which will save you more effort in the future).

If you're still not getting the hang of it, which is totally fine, let's go over the same examples differently: examining the bad habit and the trigger, root cause, consequences, and solutions.

Bad Habit 1: Telling yourself you're not enough.

- Trigger: Looking at yourself in the mirror after you've gotten ready for work.

- Root cause: Your insecurities.

- Consequences: A diminished sense of confidence.

- Solution: Adopting a more positive affirmation in its place, like "I am beautiful."

- Result: Feeling more content in life.

Bad Habit 2: Feeling broke.

- Trigger: Paying bills.

- Root cause: Not having what you perceive as enough in your bank account.

- Consequences: Continual cycles of financial problems.

- Solution: Develop a healthier relationship with money by imagining it pouring into your life from an unlimited number of places.

- Result: Your financial situation will improve.

Bad Habit 3: Getting distracted.

- Trigger: Sitting down to start working each morning.

- Root cause: Feeling overwhelmed with your to-do list.

- Consequences: Doing an inadequate job as you complete each task.

- Solution: Push all thoughts of other projects or assignments out of your head.

- Result: You will be even more productive as you put all your focus on one goal at a time.

No matter which way you best comprehend and undergo this process to start changing, or even once you're in the thick of changing a habit, it's perfectly fine to remember and repeat these steps as often as you need.

Also, like so many things mentioned in this book, please remember that overcoming hard-wired habits is a unique process that depends on you and the behavior you wish to conquer. If it takes you a few tries to figure out what combination of identifying cues, disrupting, replacing, keeping it simple, thinking long-term, and persisting when it comes to making excuses, that's okay.

Always give yourself the grace of being a human. Oh, and don't be afraid to laugh a little along the way! Life is messy and hard at times. Finding the humor in the darkness and mundane is a powerful gift.

Chapter Six

Seek Novelty

> "Be a curator of your life. Slowly cut things out until you're left only with what you love, what's necessary, and what makes you happy."
>
> –Leo Babauta

What does seeking novelty have to do with defragging your brain?

Something is *novel* when it is different, new, or unusual to you. Humans gravitate to new things. Give a baby a choice between a familiar toy and a new one and watch them reach for the new one. We've all experienced the lift that comes with finding new music we love, meeting a new friend, learning something new, buying a new outfit, or traveling somewhere we've never been.

Brain health scientists suggest that this attraction to new things was part of early humans' continued existence. The ability to notice, learn about, and adapt to new things—whether threats or rewards—increased the odds of survival.

Science also tells us that encountering new things releases dopamine, one of the feel-good neurotransmitters in our brains. Dealing with things out of our ordinary day-to-day routine is exciting. Our mood increases, we see things more positively, and we feel more motivated. We deal with stress more effectively and get more creative.

Like our ancestors, a steady diet of novelty makes us more resilient to adversity. This more positive state of mind stimulates all the benefits of an uncluttered, defragged brain.

That sounds like a lot of benefits from simple exposure to unfamiliar things, doesn't it? But it's clear that a regular diet of curiosity and learning makes us happier, healthier people.

Novelty doesn't have to mean a major change like getting a new job or expensive splurges like bungee jumping; daily doses of micro-novelty work just as well, and you can easily gain the skill of looking for or creating novel experiences.

How to Be a Novelty-Seeker

We need routines and predictability, but we must balance them with out-of-the-ordinary experiences of stimulation, appreciation, and wonder to have a zestful life. Here are a few tips for developing an eye for seeking lively experiences.

- Turn away from the screens. Most of us have plenty of screen time in our lives. Let's find life in other places.

- Spend time with children. Let them lead. Watch them experience novelty.

- Slow down. Do your regular activities slowly and see if you can notice something new. Take a walk slowly. Chew slowly. Take time to notice and experience deeply.

- Drive home by a different route.

- Brush your teeth with your non-alternate hand.

- Listen to a new kind of music, read a different genre of book, or try a new type of food.

- Seek out new groups of people.

- If you always listen to music in the car, try silence.

- If you always go out on weekends, stay home, or vice versa.

You get the idea. Develop the habit of asking yourself, "What can I do differently today? What is here that I'm not experiencing? How can I seek out something new this week?"

The funny thing is that once you begin doing something new, at some point it is no longer novel! So continually seeking new experiences of novelty is key.

Below are examples of everyday things you can do at home with your family if you have young children, with a group of friends, or if you want to discover a new hobby.

Things to Do at Home with Kids

Contrary to popular belief, there are several inexpensive and fun ways to hang out with your children (of any age) at home.

In the Kitchen

- **Have a cooking contest.** Choose different recipes or pick a limited amount of ingredients and find out who can make the best dish at the end. It'll be fun to make, eat, and then discuss after.

- **Super popcorn night.** This is kind of like a cooking contest, but it is focused just on popcorn. Each person or team starts with the same base, but they can add whatever they want. Leftover candy, crushed potato chips, drizzled chocolate, pretzels, and anything else can add whatever sugary or salty flair you're looking for. It's extra fun to do this before watching a movie together.

- **Original pizzas.** You can start with English muffins, bread, flour tortillas, or whatever you want, and then add your desired ingredients—cheese, olives, pineapple, peppers, etc. The person or team with the best creation at the end wins!

Getting Creative and Strategic

- **Costume charades.** Write down a name of different characters to create by combining old Halloween or other dress-up costumes, have each person pick one, go to town with the outfits, and then you can all guess who someone is dressed as.

- **Art Night.** Most homes have an array of art supplies somewhere. You can pull all of them out and either have designated stations (for drawing, finger painting, etc.) or just go nuts with a mixture of everything. At the end of the night, each artist can take a turn showing off their work.

- **Make movies.** What's more fun than watching a movie? Making one! We all have smartphones with video functions nowadays, and ideas can include recreating your favorite movie scene, parodying a music video, writing your own play, or creating a dance video. When you're finished, you can all watch and laugh.

- **Family puzzle.** If you have one at home, find your most complicated or biggest (meaning in size or the most pieces) and dump it out on a table. Then, have the whole family go in on it together.

- **Laser games.** We've likely all seen spy movies with a scene where someone has to bob and weave to avoid tripping off one of the lasers that are guarding a room or expensive artifact. Well, you can recreate this by tying string in all different directions in a hallway or other suitable area in your house. After it's set up, each member of the family can take a turn trying to avoid the "lasers."

STEM Activities

- **Science experiments.** There are tons of easy and enjoyable experiments for you to do with your kids. Here are some ideas (and you can find more detailed instructions and other projects online).

    - **Lava lamps**. When you pour vegetable oil into water and then add an Alka-Seltzer tablet, a blob of oil will move around.

    - **Homemade slime**. There are many ways to make it, but one of the easiest is by combining glue, Borax, and your child's favorite color in the form of food coloring.

    - **Dancing raisins**. This one requires three supplies: sparkling water (or club soda), raisins, and a clear drinking glass. (This one is most impressive to a younger crowd).

- ◦ **"Magic" milk.** A drop or two of dish soap will cause food coloring to "dance" in a shallow bowl of milk.

  ◦ **Elephant toothpaste** (aka "impressively large foam"). This experiment helps kids understand catalysts and chemical reactions. It requires a combination of dish soap, yeast, hydrogen peroxide, warm water, and sanding sugar (for coloring).

  ◦ **Grow crystals.** It's easy to grow crystals using Borax on seashells. You can also grow salt crystals or salt crystals.

- **LEGO.** Get out all of your LEGO bricks (including the parts from different sets, if available) and have competitions to see who can build the best castle, house, etc.

- **Video Games.** It might seem counterproductive to encourage your kids to play even *more* video games, but some are age-appropriate and fun for the whole family. Plus, several involve game play, so you can all play together. Keep track of who wins and have a special prize for them.

Sports

- **Sumo wrestling.** If you don't have carpet, put a bunch of rugs or blankets down in the middle of your living room or basement. Stuff your clothes with as many pillows as you can before jumping into your opponent.

- **Family yoga.** Get the whole family into comfy clothes and lie down mats or blankets and play a "yoga for kids" video. This can help them get their wiggles and giggles out before bed.

Miscellaneous

- **Saran-wrap game.** This one can be a little pricey if you aren't careful, but a stop at the nearest dollar store may help. You just need to get a bunch of knickknacks (candy, gift cards, cash, etc.) and wrap them in different layers of Saran wrap until you have a big ball. Then, have your family sit around the counter or table, and take timed turns trying to unravel as many goodies as they can while wearing mittens.

Stay-at-Home Activities to Do with Friends

Although there are several activities listed above that you can do with your friends (especially the cooking contests, costume charades, making movies, and Saran wrap game), here are a few more that a group of adults might enjoy. Of course, as long as the subject is appropriate, kids can always get involved too.

In the Kitchen

- **Charcuterie board night.** It seems like charcuterie boards are all the rage these days, and it can be really fun to host themed nights where each person is given a different aspect of a theme (like a particular color, for instance) and tasked with coming up with entire boards that fit it. Sticking with the color example, assign each person a different one—pink, yellow, red, purple, etc.—and then they have to think of different foods that are that color.

- **Friendsgiving or Galentine's Day.** These nights are around holidays that are usually spent with your family or significant other. But celebrating with friends is also really fun and a great way to show your platonic appreciation for someone. More often than not, it will be like a potluck, with everyone bringing their own dishes to share.

- **International food night or cooking class.** If your friend group is like most, there are probably people with all different cultural backgrounds in it. So it can be fun to have each person make and bring a dish from their heritage to share. Or, if you want to learn how to make a specific dish from a friend's culture, ask him or her to teach you and others how to make it.

Music and Arts

- **Yard-chella.** Set up a bunch of pillows in your backyard and either have friends take turns DJing or stream events from the actual festival while you and your friends lounge around or dance.

- **Karaoke.** You don't need a karaoke machine for this. All you need to do is pull up lyric videos on the internet and take turns with friends singing.

- **Movie-themed nights.** Pick a particular movie (some fun ones are *Grease, The Princess Bride, The Goonies, Barbie, Superbad, The Greatest Showman, Mean Girls,* or any other popular movie that has a diverse cast of characters) and have every guest dress like a character in it for a viewing party. If the weather is good and you have the equipment, it can be even more fun to project the movie on the side or your house or garage and watch it outside.

- **Wine and paint nights.** You can find painting tutorials online to project for a whole group of people. All you need is wine, canvases, paint, brushes, and easels.

- **Throwback parties.** This is like the movie-themed nights, but you can pick a decade or a certain style of dress (like "emo" night, for example), have guests dress appropriately, and play associated music for them.

Miscellaneous

- **Derby parties.** Most people can't attend the actual Kentucky Derby, but you can most likely get a fancy hat or fascinator, some suspenders, and a bow tie and host a derby party right from your home. You can watch it on TV, and some apps let you bet on the races.

- **Murder mystery parties.** Like several others on this list, this one often requires an element of dress up—you can assign your friends certain roles, have them dress to fit it, and then develop a fun night of intrigue revolving around a fake murder case. At the end, reveal which character was responsible. Some people hire actors to fill in roles, but you don't have to.

- **Spa days.** Especially if you're feeling stressed or know one or more of your friends is, coming together and painting each other's nails, giving each other facials, and just overall relaxing can be just the ticket.

Establishing a New Hobby

Finding a new hobby is a great way to invite novelty into your life. It will challenge and stimulate you to master new skills, which in turn increases your confidence and self-esteem. A new sense of purpose can lessen boredom and improve your focus. The good stress of challenging yourself is good for your health and your brain. You may even be exposed to a new group of people.

There are seemingly endless choices around hobbies. Unless there's something you've always wanted to try, it can be easy to feel overwhelmed. Let's look at a process for narrowing down your choices and getting some clarity about what you want.

What's Your Goal?

Think about what you hope to gain from engaging in this hobby. For example, you might want to make new friends, enrich your creativity, make your body stronger, bond with your kids, etc. You might even want to gain skills that can benefit your career or make you money in other contexts, like learning a new language. Having a goal or two in mind will help guide you to a satisfying choice. You won't meet many people by doing puzzles alone at home, but you could by joining a book club.

- Take some time to jot down some general life goals you have right now.
    - As an example, let's say I want to meet new people and keep my brain healthy.

- Note some activities or skills that attract you. Dream big! Don't worry about practicality at this point; just write down things that perk your interest or you've always wanted to experience.
    - My list includes African safari, hiking in the mountains, and knitting.

- Break down those attractions into what you actually desire. *Why* do you want to travel to Italy? What exactly would riding horses add to your life?

- A safari reflects my love of wildlife, and when I boil it down, what attracts me is the sense of wonder I get when I see those animals.

- Hiking in the mountains is similar—wonder and beauty—but also includes moving my body and being with friends.

- I've always wanted to learn to knit. What I imagine it would bring is competency, peacefulness, creativity, producing something I could gift, and the satisfaction of mastering a skill.

• Now you have a list of the substance of what you want. You may not be able to afford a horse, but you can look at different ways to achieve the essence of what you want—the sense of connection with nature, adventure, relationship with animals, or whatever it is for you.

- Even though I can't go to Africa and don't live near mountains, now I know that I want wonder, beauty, being with friends, and to master new skills that include creativity and productivity.

• Look for hobbies in which at least some of those opportunities interface with the life goals you mentioned in the first step.

- Because I want to meet new friends and keep my brain healthy, I'll consider in-person knitting classes, since learning to knit will be great brain exercise. For social and physical workouts, hiking clubs would be great. My area also has volunteer opportunities around local wildlife, so those groups are also worth a look.

- Now I have three new hobbies to research. If none of them work out, I can come back and do this whole exercise again to uncover more possibilities.

Once you have identified goals and know the essence of what you're attracted to, you can get practical. Two of the biggest considerations are time and money. Let's stimulate your thinking by considering a few hobbies and the range of time and money they might require.

Crafts

- **Crocheting/knitting**. As long as you are smart about the type of yarn you buy, this can be a cost-effective hobby. You can also dedicate as much time as you want to it.

- **Drawing**. All you need to draw is some paper, a few pencils, colored pencils, and a good eraser. If you need inspiration, you can either sit outside or look up an image online. Even if you just want to color in adult coloring books, you can find them for reasonable prices.

- Other crafts, like scrapbooking, building LEGO sets, quilting, and painting, can be more time- and cost-consuming. But with added investment comes more pay-off in novelty, skill-building, and challenge!

Exercise

- **Hiking**. In general, hiking trails are free to walk on, and all you need is a good pair of shoes and water to keep you hydrated.

- **Roller-skating or blading**. You can get inexpensive skates on Amazon (although they might not be the best quality), and you can skate around your neighborhood or on some trials for free.

- **Jump!** Although some of us see this exercise as something children do, it's also a great cardiovascular activity for adults. Good sneakers and a jump rope or a mini-trampoline are cost-effective avenues to fun.

- **Yoga or Pilates**. You can find free classes on YouTube to follow along with. And you can dedicate as much time as you want to them—following the entire video or not. You'll need a few low-cost items such as a yoga mat, blocks, etc. Attending community classes will bring you a new community to interact with.

- **Crossfit** or gym memberships are more expensive, but you'll be exposed to a community of people who share your interest and will support yours.

- **Dance classes** are available from free online subscriptions and community gatherings to paid in-person classes and even tournaments.

- **Horseback riding** is expensive and time-consuming—and for some people, it's a long-term dream.

- **Downhill skiing or snowboarding** is similarly expensive. It's a thrilling way to be in nature during a season that can be gray, cold, and depressing. There are less costly ways to be there as well; many ski areas have free sledding hills or access to snowshoeing or cross-country skiing areas.

- **Golf and scuba-diving** are equipment-, time-, training-, and cost-intense. On the other hand, setting up a putting green, enjoying mini-golf, or snorkeling all offer some of the same pleasures!

Enrichment of the Mind

- **Language apps**. There are plenty of applications available on your phone or computer, like Duolingo (free) and Babbel (for an annual subscription). Further, you only have to spend short chunks of your time on lessons (typically fifteen to thirty minutes, but you can do more if you want).

- **Writing**. When writing—a book, a blog post, or anything else—you generally just need access to a computer with a word processor downloaded onto it and the ability to type. And even if you don't have that, you can always go the old-fashioned way and write on paper with a pencil or pen.

- **Reading**. Between libraries, Little Free Libraries in neighborhoods, swapping books with friends, and second-hand bookstores, reading is a low-cost pleasure, and you can give it however much time you have, even if it's ten minutes on the bus to work.

- **Classes**. If there's a specific topic or skill that captivates you, options range from community classes (check out your town's parks and recreation department) to community-college or other in-person classes. There are many free educational resources online as well; a website called Open Culture lists over 1,700 free university courses available online. Check out Crash Course, an online library of AP high school courses for free.

- **Museums** are great sources of novelty, wonder, and stimulation! They can be expensive, but most offer free days or discounts at different points during the year.

Whether you take up a new hobby or encounter novelty with friends or family, defrag your brain by inviting in newness. When you do, you'll find benefits that impact every area of your life positively, and you'll feel more alive.

Chapter Seven

Manage Your Mood

> "Worrying does not take away tomorrow's troubles. It takes away today's peace."
>
> –Randy Armstrong

We all have difficult moods and times when life is more challenging than others. Part of learning to defrag your mind means gaining skills to cope with those times. In this chapter, we'll look at five tools you can build to have at your disposal.

Many people struggle with depression, which goes beyond normal moodiness and is a mental health issue. If you think you are depressed, please do not hesitate to reach out to your doctor to discuss treatments, therapies, or medications that may be able to help you avoid struggle and potential detrimental changes to your brain.

These five mood-management tools, however—physical activity, rewarding yourself, proper diet and nutrition, positive social interactions, and therapy—are useful to everyone.

Physical Activity

Both aerobic exercise (like walking, running, dancing, rowing, swimming, playing tennis, etc.) and anaerobic exercise (lifting weights) raise your heart rate and cause the release of endorphins or "feel good" chemicals in your brain.

In addition, your increased heart rate triggers the release of norepinephrine, a chemical that helps your brain deal with stress more effectively. Exercise also helps increase the blood flow to your brain.

All of this in turn benefits and impacts all your cellular functions, improving your concentration, regulating sleep, and boosting your mood.

However, only aerobic exercise changes the amount of oxygen your body uses for energy. As such, the American Heart Association and the American College of Sports Medicine recommend at least thirty minutes of aerobic activity five days a week. It's good to add anaerobic exercises to that as well. The Centers for Disease Control and Prevention recommends getting at least two sessions of strength training per week.

Tips for Staying Active

How do you stay motivated to work out? Try these.

- **Find an activity you like doing.** If you're just starting, feel free to experiment with different kinds of exercise to find some you genuinely like. Going forward, you'll look forward to doing something you enjoy.

- **Go at your own pace.** Again, if you're just starting or are getting back to exercise after a break of some kind, feel free to take things slow at first. Beginning a new routine with short intervals of an activity sends positive feedback to your brain. You're more likely to stick with a fitness plan when you start slow.

- **Use tech tools.** There are plenty of devices (like a Fitbit or Apple Watch) that you can wear to track your steps and other or activity. Plus, there are a lot of free or low-cost apps you can download to help track your progress.

    - **Caliber**. The free version allows you to log your workouts or create custom workout programs for you, has a library of 500 exercises with extensive overviews of each one, and records and charts your strength progress and body metrics; the premium subscription includes all of that and one-on-one and group training.

    - **Nike Training Club**. It's free and gives you expert tips on nutrition, recovery, and weight loss while also offering live or on-demand classes.

    - **Map My Fitness**. The free version gives you extensive GPS tracking and other features; the premium subscription version comes with heart rate analyses, power output, running cadence, and more.

    - **Jetfit**. The free version allows you to log and track your workouts while giving users access to an expansive library of exercises and a limited number of exercise routines; the subscription provides you access to more audio workouts.

    - **ClassPass**. The free version has a database of workout videos that vary from strength training to high-intensity workouts; the subscription plan allows you to search and participate in local classes—HIIT, boot camp, kettlebell classes, plus salon appointments.

- **FitOn**. The free version gives you access to tons of guided workout videos; the premium option allows you to add music to spice up your workout, personalize meal plans, and offline downloads to workouts.

- **Hevy**. The free version comes with a robust library of exercises, allows you to log your workouts, and has a social media aspect; a pro version is also available.

Treating Yourself

We all have that one little thing that brightens our spirits, be it lipstick, a book, a piece of chocolate cake, a cup of coffee, a bouquet of flowers, or an outfit for a furry friend. Treating yourself when you're feeling down can improve your mood because when we treat ourselves, we feel happy, fulfilled, and contented, all of which boosts self-esteem. Basically, after you, as Tom and Donna on *Parks and Recreation* would say, "Treat yo self," your mindset changes for the better. So, if you're feeling a little down, decide what your special little treat is, and get it!

However, please make sure that you are not confusing treats with fixes. Aim for modest amounts of a treat that make you feel better and not worse—small things as often as you feel you need them. This means you aren't drowning yourself in alcohol, sweets, or anything else that's harmful to you when you feel stressed, sad, or overwhelmed.

Proper Diet and Nutrition

From the time we are kids, we are told that proper nutrition is the secret to keeping our bodies healthy and strong. But many of us aren't told that your diet is just as important for the well-being of your mind as it is for your body. In fact, a well-balanced diet can help us think clearly, be more alert, improve our concentration, and elongate our attention span.

On the flip side, an inadequate diet can lead to fatigue, impaired decision-making, can slow down reaction time, and can cause aggravation, stress, and depression.

So why don't we all eat healthy diets? So many people struggle with this important area of defragging your mind. Let's look at why it can be difficult and how we can support ourselves in striving for health in mind and body.

Where it Gets Tricky

One of the biggest impacts on health in today's society is the reliance on processed foods, which are high in flour and sugars and train the brain to crave more of them over nutrient-rich foods like fruits and vegetables.

Processed foods are highly addictive and stimulate the dopamine centers of our brain (which are associated with pleasure and reward). To stop craving unhealthy foods, you need to stop eating them. Interestingly enough, when you remove added sugars and refined carbohydrates from your diet, you change the physiology of your brain.

Anxiety and Depression

Sugar and processed foods can lead to inflammation in the body and brain that contributes to mood disorders like anxiety and depression.

One reason this can be a perpetuating cycle is that we most often reach for processed foods when we need a quick pick-me-up when we're upset or stressed (remember what we said about thinking in terms of minimalism when treating yourself—you don't want to eat too much candy, cookies, cake, ice cream, etc.). Another is that we commonly eat too much or too little when we're feeling overwhelmed.

Eating too much can cause you to be sluggish and gain weight, whereas eating too little is often bad for your body and organs and can lead to exhaustion.

For optimal mental health, focus on eating plenty of fruits and vegetables (with particular favor given to dark, leafy greens for brain protection). Foods rich in omega-3 fatty acids, like salmon, nuts, seeds, and legumes (like beans and lentils) are also great food for your brain.

A Healthy Gut

We've probably all heard the saying, "You are what you eat." That's true in a sense. Scientists have focused on the strong connection in our bodies between the intestines and the brain and found that they are physically linked via the vagus nerve. The gut and brain send messages to each other; the gut influences our emotions and behavior and the brain can alter the bacteria living in the gut.

According to the American Psychological Association, bacteria in our guts produce neurochemicals that the brain uses for the regulation of our moods. In fact, it is believed that around ninety-five percent of the body's supply of serotonin (a mood stabilizer) is produced by the bacteria in our gut, and stress is thought to suppress it.

Mindful Eating

Mindful eating is a really important way to go about living your life. One of the first steps to having a well-balanced diet is to pay attention to the way you feel when you eat certain things. Nutritionists recommend keeping a food journal to record what, where, and when you eat to gain insight into your eating patterns.

We've already talked about over- and undereating, but it bears addressing again. After keeping a journal for a while, you'll be able to look back when you feel nervous or stressed out and see if that's one of your triggers to overeat or undereat.

If it's to overeat, it may be helpful to stop what you're doing and instead write down how you're feeling (this will help you discover the root of the problem). And if it is to undereat, it might help if you schedule five or six smaller meals throughout the day instead of three larger ones.

But all of this is to say that sometimes stress and depression can't be conquered alone. That's perfectly normal, and not something you should be ashamed to admit to or seek help for. Reaching out to a professional therapist or counselor isn't a sign of weakness or failure. Instead, it speaks to your bravery and commitment to success in life.

Brain Food

Your brain and nervous systems rely on nutrition to build new proteins, cells, and tissues. For your body to function effectively, it requires a variety of carbohydrates, proteins, and minerals. And to get all of those, nutritionists typically suggest you eat snacks and meals that include a variety of foods instead of eating the same meals over and over again.

In particular, there are three top foods to incorporate into your diet for the benefit of your mental health.

- Complex carbohydrates. Brown rice and starchy vegetables give you energy; quinoa, millet, beets, and sweet potatoes are more nutritious and will keep you feeling full for longer than simple carbohydrates like sugar and candy.

- Lean proteins. Good sources of protein include chicken, fish, eggs, soybeans, nuts, and seeds.

- Fatty acids (particularly monosaturated or polyunsaturated).

  - Fish (salmon, herring, sardines, and other oily, fatty fish), flaxseed oil, olive oil, chia seeds, walnuts, canola oil, sunflower oil, and avocados are all great sources of healthy fatty acids.

  - There are also other food items—like bread, cereal, flour, pasta, peanut butter, oatmeal, pumpkin seeds, flour tortillas, and packaged pizza—that may have omega-3 fatty acids added to them.

  - Leafy green vegetables and other vegetables are good sources of ALA, a form of omega-3 fatty acids. They include Brussels sprouts, kale, spinach, broccoli, and cauliflower.

  - If you have a baby, you may want to look for infant cereals, formula, and jars of baby food with the omega-3 fatty acid, DHA. Research has shown that it helps their brains develop.

  - Other omega-3-enhanced products include supplements, vitamins, meal replacement bars, protein powders, and weight loss shakes.

Health Eating Tips

Here are some things to think about the next time you eat or go to the grocery store.

- Avoid processed and sugar-filled snacks (like potato chips, candy, and soft drinks) because they are bad for you and will contribute to ups and downs in your energy levels. (Don't be fooled: it may feel like sugar energizes you, but that rush is only temporary).

- Consume plenty of healthy fats (like olive oil, coconut oil, and avocado) to support your brain function.

- Opt for a healthy snack (like fruits, nuts, hard-boiled eggs, baked sweet potatoes, or edamame) when hunger strikes. They will give you more energy than any packaged product can.

- Develop a healthy shopping list and be diligent in sticking to it once in the store. It's easy to grab your favorite bag of candy or bottle of soda. But you can resist them! We know you can.

- Don't shop when you're hungry. This makes it more likely that you'll stray from your list and make unhealthy impulse selections.

- Think about where and when you eat. For instance, eating in front of the TV can be distracting and cause you to overeat. Instead, a quiet and relaxing place where you can notice the feeling, taste, and texture of your food is best.

Interacting Positively with Others

The number and strength of your relationships impact your physical and mental health.

Having positive social connections with other people has proven to be linked to lower rates of anxiety and depression and higher self-esteem, greater empathy, trust, and cooperation.

When it comes to your physical well-being, having strong friendships and relationships with partners and family members make your immune system stronger. Therefore, it can help you avoid or recover from disease and, in doing so, lengthen your life.

A cool thing about all of this is that it's reciprocal for everyone involved. When you have a strong, healthy relationship with someone, you are providing them with the same benefits that you're getting from that connection.

Three Kinds of Connections

There are three types of connections that most people share with others.

- **Intimate connections**. These are relationships with people who love and care for you, such as your romantic partner, friends, and family.

- **Relational connections**. These relationships are with people who you see regularly and share an interest with, such as your friends from work or the baristas you see every morning.

- **Collective connections**. You share these with people who share memberships and affiliations with you, such as people of the same faith or who vote the same as you.

Ask yourself: do you have meaningful, long-term relationships in all three of these areas? If not, you might want to consider the following:

- Do you tend to only stick with old friendships and bonds?

- Do you avoid people from your past and fear others getting close to you?

If you answered yes to either of those questions, or if you otherwise feel like you could benefit from either making new friends or reinvigorating old friendships, one of the first steps to consider is to reach out to people you already know—coworkers, neighbors, and friends from school. Call them and make plans. If you're looking to meet new people, ask them to bring their friends along.

Next, consider starting a conversation with someone you see every day (like people you see at the gym or on the bus), joining a rec sports team, or volunteering. However, when meeting new people, please be sure to be safe and meet in a public place until you get to know them and build trust.

Further, please be aware that not every way of making new friends is going to work out for everyone. So, if your first attempt fails, keep trying with other methods and people.

Impact of Loneliness

On the other end of the spectrum, there are health and mental consequences that come with being lonely or isolated from others. It can lead to disrupted sleep patterns, elevated blood pressure, and increased cortisol. It can also lower your immune system and increase your chances of developing antisocial behavior, depression, and suicidal ideation.

Younger and older people are both more susceptible to becoming lonely and suffering from some of these risk factors.

The older generation is unfortunately sometimes forgotten by younger family members. It doesn't help that many elderly people lose their mobility, so it gets harder and harder for them to make the effort to see and be around people. However, older individuals who are well connected with friends and family are said to have a better quality of life, be more satisfied, have a lower risk of having a stroke, dementia, and other mental decline, and need less domestic support.

People in their teens and early twenties who do not make connections with their peers have an increased risk of obesity, inflammation, and high blood pressure.

Therapy

If you go through all of the motions listed above and still find that you're struggling with your mental health, please trust a professional to help you. As we've said, there is absolutely no shame in doing so.

You may not realize it, but there are many different kinds of therapy. Here are some of them.

Accelerated Experiential Dynamic Psychotherapy (AEDP)

AEDP is a form of talk therapy that aims to help people overcome trauma, loss, or other serious emotional challenges. It posits that humans are wired for resilience and have an inborn ability to cope with emotional pain; however, many people who have undergone trauma are unable to access the skills that allow them to navigate their emotional changes. AEDP aims to help clients draw out these coping mechanisms.

> **When it's used.** To treat childhood trauma and post-traumatic stress disorder (PTSD).
>
> **What to expect.** AEDP is an active therapeutic modality, meaning that therapists participate in discussions and explorations with the client rather than taking on a more detached approach that is typical of other types of therapy.

How it works. The founder of AEDP, a psychologist named Diana Fosha, argues that trauma or other painful emotions can lead to "utter aloneness." AEDP undoes that aloneness through a supportive and encouraging relationship with one's therapist.

What to look for in an AEDP therapist: You may want to find therapists who have had specific training and certification processes in Accelerated Experiential Dynamic Psychotherapy. If not, make sure you find a professional that you can feel comfortable talking with because that—having a strong connection with your therapist—is a huge component of this type of therapy.

Acceptance and Commitment Therapy (ACT)

ACT is an action-oriented approach to psychotherapy that stems from traditional behavior therapy and cognitive behavioral therapy (which are both discussed below). Clients going through ACT learn to stop avoiding, denying, and struggling with their inner emotions and instead accept that these deeper feelings are appropriate responses to certain situations that should not prevent them from moving forward in life.

When it is used. To treat several mental and physical conditions—including anxiety, depression, obsessive-compulsive disorders, psychosis, eating disorders, substance use disorders, workplace stress, and chronic pain.

What to expect. After working with a therapist, you'll learn to listen to your own self-talk (the way you talk about yourself), specifically in terms of traumatic events, problematic relationships, physical limitations, and other challenges. Then you'll decide if a problem requires immediate action and change.

How it works. The theory behind ACT is that it is counterproductive to try to control emotions or psychological experiences, and that suppression of these feelings ultimately leads to more distress.

What to look for in an ACT therapist: There is no special certification for ACT practitioners. Instead, look for experienced therapists, social workers, professional counselors, or other mental health professionals with additional training in ACT, which is obtained through peer counseling, workshops, and other training programs. In addition, it's important that you work with someone who you feel comfortable being around and opening up to.

Adlerian Therapy (AKA Individual Psychotherapy)

This is short-term, goal-oriented, and positive psychodynamic therapy based on the theories of Alfred Adler, a colleague of Sigmund Freud. Adler focused much of his research on feelings of inferiority versus superiority, discouragement, and a sense of belonging in the context of one's community and society at large. According to Adler, feelings of inferiority can result in neurotic behavior. However, in the right setting, it can also be used as motivation to strive for success.

When it's used. Adlerian therapy can be applied successfully to any type of psychological disorder or mental illness. It can also be used in conjunction with other types of therapy. It can also be applied to children, adolescents, adults, individuals, couples, families, and other groups.

How it works. One of the core principals of this kind of therapy is that individual behavior must be explored within the context of a client's sense of fitting in with their community and society at large. Adlerian therapists often work in schools, clinics, corporate offices, and other community settings and help to create learning environments that provide a sense of belonging and respect for all.

What to expect. Adlerian therapy is done in four stages: Engagement, which involves developing a relationship between patient and therapist; Assessment, which involves learning about the patient and their present challenges; Insight, in which the therapist uses his or her insight to uncover why the patient acts the way they do and help them see themselves and their circumstances differently; and Reorientation, which involves changes in attitudes, beliefs, and lifestyle choices.

What to look for in an Adlerian therapist. This type of therapist is a licensed psychotherapist with a master's degree or doctorate and specialized training/experience in an Adlerian approach. The North American Society of Adlerian Psychology and other academic institutions offer certifications and degree programs. Please also note that other professionals such as nurses, teachers, and counselors may also incorporate Adlerian principles into their work.

Affirmative Therapy (or LBGTQ+ Affirmative Therapy)

This is a therapeutic approach that validates and advocates for the needs of sexual and gender minority individuals. It celebrates and validates their identities while acknowledging the stigma and obstacles they face.

When it's used. Primarily used to treat LGBTQ+ individuals who benefit from therapy that takes into account a thoughtful and supportive understanding of gender and sexuality, it aims to help clients process and cope with the challenges that come with being a part of the LGBTQ+ community. However, it also helps with mental challenges that are not the result of gender and sexuality, such as relationships, self-esteem, careers, etc.

How it works. Sexual and gender minority individuals often face challenges of prejudice and bias that lead to stress, anxiety, and other mental health issues. Affirmative therapy provides a supportive environment to deal with and process those experiences.

What to expect. Patients should be open and willing to discuss their experiences and address their mental health challenges with a therapist who is experienced and informed on LGBTQ+ issues and ready to celebrate their identity.

What to look for in an affirmative therapist. A good affirmative therapist is self-aware, self-reflective, and has thought deeply about their upbringing, their beliefs, and their potential biases. Of course, they must also be educated on gender and sexuality.

Animal-Assisted Therapy

This therapeutic intervention incorporates animals such as horses, dogs, cats, and even birds into a treatment plan.

When it's used. Animal-assisted therapy can be helpful for individuals or groups experiencing stress, anxiety, depression, autism, ADHD, addiction, schizophrenia; emotional and behavioral problems in children; Alzheimer's disease, and some medical conditions. Patients should not undergo this type of therapy if they dislike, fear, or are allergic to animals.

How it works. Animal-assisted therapy is based on the deep bond that can develop between people and animals. Patients can experience a sense of calm, comfort, or safety from the animals. Also, some report developing more self-worth, trust, stabilized emotions, and improvement in communication, self-regulation, and socialization skills.

What to expect. Depending on the nature of your therapy, you might keep a dog, cat, or other pet at home for emotional support, or you may go to a facility where animals such as horses are kept, and learn how to ride and care for them.

What to look for in an animal-assisted therapist. As with other kinds of therapy, you want to find an animal-assisted therapist you trust and feel comfortable around. You may also want to ask a potential therapist the following questions: How would they help with your particular concerns? Have they dealt with this type of problem before? What is their process like? What is their general timeline for treatment?

Applied Behavior Analysis (ABA)

ABA is frequently applied to children with autism and other developmental disorders and focuses on imparting skills in specific, tailored domains of functioning, such as social skills, communication, academic and learning skills, motor dexterity, hygiene and grooming, and more.

When is it used. As mentioned, ABA is commonly practiced for children with autism.

How it works. A trained behavior analyst assesses a person's needs and abilities before designing a program of therapy with specific goals and focused skills in mind, including communication, self-care, play and leisure, motor skills, and learning and academic skills. ABA therapists use the following techniques.

- **Discrete Trial Training** (DTT). Usually conducted in a one-on-one session, the therapist breaks skills into small units for the patient and teaches them one by one with the appropriate reinforcements until the skill is mastered.

- **Modeling**. A technique in which the therapist presents an example of the desired behavior, either personally demonstrating it or providing a video or audio recording of somebody else doing the desired behavior. After that, the patient is asked to mimic the target behavior.

- **Picture Exchange Communication System** (PECS). PECS involves the use of pictures to teach communication and vocabulary skills to children. The child, who is working with a set of cards having pictures of food or other objects, gives the therapist the card that represents the desired object. Then the therapist provides the object shown in the picture.

- **Reinforcement Systems**. These methods teach children the consequences of engaging in specific activities and behaviors. The goal is for the desired behaviors and activities to be repeated in the future. An example is the token system. The child earns tokens as a reward for engaging in the desired activity. Then, when they've earned enough tokens, they can play a video game, watch a show, etc.

What to expect. Clients and therapist together determine which behaviors they need to change, set goals and expected outcomes, establish ways to measure changes and improvements, evaluate where they are now, learn new skills and/or learn how to avoid negative behaviors, regularly review progress, and decide whether or not further behavior modification is necessary.

What to look for in an ABA therapist. Most states now have regulations requiring specific licensure for ABA therapists.

Art Therapy

Creative techniques such as drawing, painting, collage, coloring, or sculpting help people express themselves creatively and examine the psychological and emotional undertones of their art. With the guidance of a professional art therapist, clients decipher the nonverbal messages, symbols, and metaphors found in their work. This can lead to a better understanding of their feelings and behaviors.

When it's used With individuals, couples, and groups in a variety of settings, including private counseling, hospitals, wellness centers, correction facilities, senior centers, and other community settings. Contrary to popular belief, no artistic talent is necessary for art therapy to succeed. It can help people who suffer from or who want to address certain issues, like emotion exploration, self-esteem problems, stress, anxiety, depression, trauma, grief, personality disorders, physical illnesses, and disabilities.

How it works. Art therapy is founded on the belief that self-expression through artistic creation has therapeutic value for those who are healing or seeking a deeper understanding of themselves. Art therapists are trained to understand the roles that color, texture, and various art media can play in the therapeutic process and how these tools can help to reveal one's thoughts and feelings.

> **What to expect**. Your first few sessions will likely consist of talking to the art therapist about why you're seeking that specific form of therapy. Then you'll come up with a treatment plan together that involves some form of artwork. Once you begin creating, the therapist may observe you and ask certain questions about it.
>
> **What to look for** in an art therapist. The initials ATR after a therapist's name indicates that he or she is registered with the Art Therapy Credentials Board (ATCB). The initials ATR-BC mean that the therapist is not only registered but has passed an examination to become board-certified by the ATCB.

Attachment-Based Therapy

ABT is a brief process-oriented form of counseling. The client-therapist relationship is based on developing or rebuilding trust and focuses on expressing emotions. This type of approach to therapy looks at the connection between an infant's early attachment experiences with primary caregivers, most commonly parents, and the person's ability to develop normal and healthy relationships later as an adult.

> **When it's used**. ABT can be used in individual, family, couple, and group therapy with both children and adults to help people mend or overcome fractured family relationships. Those who may benefit from this type of therapy include adopted children, children in foster care, children of depressed parents, children who have experienced abuse or trauma, particularly at the hands of a caregiver, and adolescents who are depressed or suicidal.
>
> **How it works**. Without a healthy foundation of love and care, babies may grow fearful, confused, insecure, and sometimes grow into depressed or suicidal adolescents. In theory, by forming a

trusting relationship with parental figures or with the therapist, the client is better prepared to form strong relationships with others.

What to expect. If the client is an adolescent, the therapist will work with the individual alone before working with the family as a group. If the client is an adult, the therapist aims to help the client overcome the effects of negative early attachment difficulties by establishing a secure bond between the therapist and the client.

What to look for in an attachment-based therapist. A qualified attachment-based therapist is a psychologist, psychotherapist, clinical social worker, marriage and family therapist, or other licensed clinician with an attachment-based treatment approach and experience.

Behavioral Activation (BA)

BA is a form of short-term outpatient therapy that engages individuals in rewarding activities of their own choosing as a way to counter the negative feelings and withdrawal that are typical of depression (and sometimes anxiety). BA is a basic component of cognitive behavioral therapy, but when it is applied intensively, it is also used and incorporated into many other types of therapy.

When it is used. BA is suitable for people with depression or anxiety who are not at immediate risk of self-harm and who do not want or can't take medications to relieve symptoms.

How it works. It is based on the knowledge that inactivity leads to depression, which leads to more inactivity and deeper depression. BA offers a way of feeling better quickly, directing stimulating improvement in mood through action.

What to expect. It usually takes place in weekly sessions for anywhere from eight to twenty-four weeks depending on the severity of symptoms and response to treatment.

What to look for in a BA therapist: a BA therapist is a licensed mental health professional who has additional training and experience in BA or a community health worker who has undergone training in BA. All CBT therapists have had some training in BA.

Bibliotherapy

Bibliotherapy employs books and other forms of literature, typically alongside more traditional therapy types. The books a therapist may recommend can range from fiction, philosophy, self-help, and memoirs.

When it's used. Bibliotherapy can be applied to patients suffering from anxiety, depression, or other mood disorders, those struggling with trauma or addiction, or those who are going through grief, a divorce, or other life struggles. It can also be practiced in individual or group therapy sessions or without the guidance of a therapist at all.

How it works. A bibliotherapist will recommend books based on the preferred modality and the patient's specific challenges. The patient reads the book or completes a workbook exercise as determined by the therapist. The process may occur in four stages: Identification, in which the reader connects with a character in the text and identifies with their problems and goals; Catharsis, in which the reader experiences the character's emotions, struggles, and hopes form a safe, removed position; Insight, in which the reader recognizes similarities between the characters or situations in the text and the reader's circumstances and applies ideas from the text to the reader's life; and Universalization, in which the reader realizes they are not alone and that others have experienced similar challenges and have found ways to navigate them.

What to expect. Extra work (i.e., reading) in between sessions with your therapist.

What to look for in a bibliotherapist. It may be helpful for you to learn about a therapist's primary modality and discuss how bibliotherapy is incorporated into one of their treatment plans. Further, some organizations, like the International Federation for Biblio/Poetry Therapy, offer certifications for interested practitioners and have set guidelines for the practice of bibliotherapy.

Biofeedback

Biofeedback involves monitoring a person's psychological state and sending information about it back to that individual.

When it's used. Biofeedback can be helpful in addressing a range of challenges and disorders, including anxiety, stress, trauma, insomnia, tension and migraine headaches, IBS and constipation, urinary incontinence, and some pain conditions.

How it works. By harnessing real-time information on one's bodily state and demonstrating how it connects to conscious behaviors—such as thinking about certain images, breathing in a certain way, or relaxing muscles—biofeedback therapy is designed to help patients take more control over the functioning of their bodies.

What to expect. A therapist may use electronic sensors that attach to a patient's skin or fingers or a belt that wraps around the waist to provide feedback on the patient's physiological state, which is presented in the form of visuals or sounds. Typical sessions last up to an hour, and during them, the therapist will explain to you what he or she is tracking.

What to look for in a biofeedback therapist. Please consult with your doctor or healthcare provider for a referral to a licensed clinician who can offer biofeedback therapy.

Couples Therapy

Couples therapy aims to help romantic partners address relationship conflicts, improve communication, and increase affection and empathy for one another.

When it's used. Couples therapy is used for a variety of reasons, often including communication challenges, frequent or intense conflicts, persistent disagreements about finances, child-rearing, the division of labor, and other concerns, or challenges related to sex and intimacy (including infidelity).

How it works. A therapist will work as an impartial third-party and help couples navigate and identify problems that are keeping them stuck. Also, the "neutral space" of the therapist's room can be a safe haven for the couple to share their emotions, hopes, and fears. The goal is for both individuals to have a greater sense of compassion for themselves and each other.

What to expect. Expectations depend on the issues that drove the couple to seek help, the approach(es) employed by the therapist, and the unique personal preferences and dynamics of the couple. However, couples can expect to spend time sharing their concerns, identifying the emotions they feel toward their partner and the relationship, exploring personal history (both the individual partners' personal history and their shared history as a couple), and learning new skills, such as anger management techniques, conflict resolution, and joint problem-solving. Most couples therapy sessions occur with both partners present. In some cases, therapists conduct individual sessions with one or both partners to gain a better understanding of their unique situations.

What to look for in a couples therapist. A licensed mental health professional—a psychologist, clinical social worker, or marriage and family therapist who has completed training in couple-focused therapy. Many couples therapists have sought additional certifications from organizations like the American Association for Marriage and Family Therapy (AAMFT) or the American Association of Sexuality Educators, Counselors, and Therapists (AASECT).

Dance Therapy (aka Dance/Movement Therapy or DMT)

This is a mental health treatment that uses dance and other forms of physical movement to improve someone's emotional and psychological functioning.

When it's used. DMT can be conducted individually or in a group setting, and it can be used to treat children, adolescents, adults, and the elderly. It helps people who face a variety of conditions and challenges, including anxiety, autism, dementia, depression, interpersonal issues—such as family conflict, domestic violence, low self-esteem—and more. Further, it can be used on its own or in conjunction with another type of therapy.

How it works. The mind and body are known to be closely connected, and movement of any kind has long been thought to bring therapeutic benefits. Dance therapy aims to strengthen the connection between the brain and the body by allowing authentic, non-verbal expression of emotions in a safe, non-judgmental environment.

What to expect. Dance therapy often starts with a warm-up, a verbal check-in, or both. The therapist and client might decide on a "theme" to explore that session (based on the client's needs or a program designed by the therapist). During the session itself, the therapist will guide the client through dance or other forms of movement that are aimed at expressing their internal emotional state.

What to look for in a dance therapist. In the United States, dance therapists are overseen by an organization known as the American Dance Therapy Association (ADTA). According to the ADTA, dance therapists should have a minimum of a master's degree as well as specific credentials called the Registered Dance/Movement Therapist (R-DMT). Therapists who go further with their training receive credentials as a Board-Certified Dance/Movement Therapist (BC-DMT).

Dialectical Behavior Therapy (DBT)

DBT is a structured program of psychotherapy with a strong educational component designed to provide skills for managing intense emotions and negotiating social relationships. The "dialectic" aspect is an acknowledgment that life is complex, and health is not a static thing but an ongoing process that requires continuous dialogue with yourself and others.

When it is used. With a strong emphasis on emotion regulation skills, DBT can aid a wide range of health conditions such as personality disorders (including borderline personality disorder), self-harming, post-traumatic stress disorder, bulimia, binge-eating disorder, depression, anxiety, substance use disorder, and bipolar disorder.

How it works. DBT is focused on emotions and how they feed ineffectual action patterns. Many elements of the therapy are aimed at teaching patients how to recognize, understand, label, and regulate their emotions and how to handle interpersonal situations that give rise to negative or painful feelings.

What to expect. A course of treatment typically consists of weekly group, skill-focused instructional meetings as well as individual therapy sessions. Individual sessions usually last an hour, and group meetings, which usually consist of four to ten people, run for an hour and a half to two hours.

What to look for in a DBT therapist. Look for a licensed mental health professional who has training and experience in DBT. However, certified DBT therapists may use the designation of CDBT.

Eye Movement Desensitization and Reprocessing Therapy (EMDR)

EMDR is a technique designed to relieve the distress associated with disturbing memories.

When it is used. EMDR was first developed as an individual treatment for people with post-traumatic stress disorder, but it has since treated many other conditions, such as anxiety disorders (including panic and phobias), depression, dissociative disorders, obsessive-compulsive disorders, and some personality disorders.

How it works. It involves recalling a specific troublesome experience while following a side-to-side visual stimulus delivered by the therapist. The resulting eye movements are thought to help reduce the emotional charge of the memory so the experience can be safely discussed, digested, and stripped of the power to trigger anxiety and/or avoidance.

What to expect. A course of treatment generally consists of six to twelve sessions, typically delivered one to two times a week, although some people may need fewer sessions. Studies have proven that one distressing memory can be (but isn't always) processed within three sessions.

What to look for in an EMDR therapist. Seek someone whom you feel safe being vulnerable in front of and Find a therapist who has training and experience in using EMDR therapy and whom you feel comfortable being vulnerable with.

Humanistic Therapy (aka Humanism)

Humanism is a form of talk therapy that focuses on a person's nature rather than assuming that groups of people with similar characteristics have the same concerns. The aim is to consider the whole person, especially their positive characteristics and potential growth, not only from the therapist's professional viewpoint but from a client's sense of their behavior.

When it's used. Humanism treats depression, anxiety and panic disorders, personality disorders, schizophrenia, addiction, and interpersonal and familial relationship concerns. It can also help people who are suffering from low self-esteem, who lack feelings of "wholeness," who are searching for personal meaning, or who are not comfortable with themselves as they are.

How it works. A core tenet of humanistic therapy is that people are inherently motivated to fulfill their internal needs and that each of us has the power to find the best solutions for ourselves and the ability to make appropriate changes in our lives (a concept known as self-actualization).

What to expect. These sessions embrace the gestalt approach, which means exploring how a person feels in the here and now rather than trying to identify and analyze the past events and traumas that led to such feelings.

What to look for in a humanistic therapist. There are no formal certifications required to practice person-centered therapy, and the humanistic approach can be incorporated into various therapy practices. However, a humanistic therapist should be a warm, empathetic, understanding, and non-judgmental person.

Hypnotherapy and Other Mindfulness Techniques

Please refer to Chapter One for information on this.

Interpersonal Therapy (IPT)

IPT is a time-limited, focused, evidence-based approach to treat mood disorders.

When it's used. IPT provides strategies to resolve problems in four key areas:
- Addressing interpersonal deficits, including social isolation or the involvement in unfulfilling relationships.
- Helping patients manage unresolved grief (if the onset of distress is linked to the death of a loved one, either recent or in the past).
- Helping with difficult transitions in life, such as retirement, divorce, or a move.
- Recommending or dealing with interpersonal disputes that emerge from conflicting expectations between partners, family members, close friends, or coworkers.

How it works. Practitioners believe that change in the social environment is a key factor in the onset of and continuation of depression. It has been shown to be comparable in efficacy to antidepressants.

What to expect. IPT typically consists of individual therapy sessions or group work completed within twelve to sixteen weeks. The treatment is structured with homework, continuous assessment, and interviews by a therapist.

What to look for in an interpersonal therapist. Since this is a newer therapy, the standards for clinical training for non-researchers (researchers being the main practitioners as of late) are still being defined. However, the International Society for Interpersonal Psychotherapy deliberates on training concerns and allows countries to develop their own credentialing and processes for interpersonal therapy.

Jungian Therapy

Based on the work of Carl Jung, this is an in-depth, analytical form of talk therapy designed to bring together the conscious and unconscious parts of the mind to help clients feel balanced and whole.

> **When it's used.** It attempts to explain all of human psychology. However, it is primarily used to treat depression, anxiety, grief, obsessive-compulsive disorder, phobias, relationship problems, low self-esteem, and a lack of purpose or direction in life. It is also said to be an appropriate therapy for anyone who wants a deeper understanding of themselves and is willing to commit to the work involved in this therapeutic process.
>
> **How it works.** Jungian therapy focuses more on the source of the problem rather than on its manifestations or symptoms. Carl Jung believed that the *shadow* (an individual's repressed experiences and memories), in combination with the *collective unconscious* (the inherent hidden beliefs that everyone in a given society at a given time has), result in an imbalance between conscious awareness and the unconscious mind that has detrimental effects on a person's emotional life. A patient must explore these forces and influences to achieve unity of the conscious and unconscious mind.
>
> **What to expect.** In Jungian therapy, a patient is asked to explore both their conscious and unconscious minds with the help of a therapist to balance the areas of their personality that are misaligned and create unity between the conscious and unconscious mind. Jung used dream analysis, word association, and art or dance therapies, among other techniques. However, it's primarily a talk therapy that includes exploring the sometimes unpleasant parts of the mind or painful experiences

to fully understand your true problems and how to fix them to the greatest extent possible.

What to look for in a Jungian therapist. Advanced training in a program accredited by the International Association for Analytical Psychology, which includes intense training that can take a therapist four to six years to complete, is necessary to become a Jungian therapist.

Mentalization-Based Therapy (MBT)

MBT is an evidence-based treatment that draws from several different psychotherapeutic approaches to treat people with borderline personality disorder and other mental health conditions. It was developed in the 1990s for people with borderline personalities.

> **When it's used**. MBT helps people who could benefit from increasing their capacity to mentalize, such as those with borderline personality disorder, antisocial personality, addictions, eating disorders, and depression.
>
> **How it works**. MBT helps patients think before they react to their feelings or the perceived feelings of others. With an improved ability to mentalize, the patient not only processes their thoughts, feelings, and related behaviors differently but also understands that another person's thoughts, feelings, and behavior may differ from their interpretations.
>
> **What to expect**. MBT practitioners work to create a safe environment for patients to begin an exploration of their feelings and those of others, ultimately developing their capacity for mentalization.

What to look for in a mindfulness-based therapist. MBT requires a mental health professional with an understanding of borderline personality disorder and some training/experience in mentalization-based interventions.

Mindfulness-Based Therapy (MBCT)

MBCT is a modified form of cognitive therapy that incorporates mindfulness practices like present-moment awareness, meditation, and breathing exercises.

When it's used. MBCT was designed to address and help those with depression, but it has since proven helpful in people with generalized anxiety disorders, bipolar disorder, general emotional distress, and addictions. Moreover, it treats physical problems like vascular disease, traumatic brain injuries, chronic pain, and fibromyalgia.

How it works. By developing a meditation practice, clients can use the technique whenever they start to feel overwhelmed by negative thoughts. Then, when sadness occurs and starts to bring up the usual negative associations that can trigger a relapse of depression, the client is equipped with tools that will help them replace their negative thinking with calmness, compassion, and positive action.

What to expect. MBCT is normally conducted within weekly group sessions led by a therapist. In about eight meetings, you will learn meditation techniques as well as basic principles of cognition, such as the relationship between the way you think and how you feel. You will also have the opportunity to learn more about your depressive condition.

What to look for in a mindfulness-based therapist. MBCT mental health professionals have additional training in mindful-based practices and techniques and are skilled in teaching these techniques to others. Universities train and certify teachers around the world.

Music Therapy

This treatment uses music within the therapeutic relationship to help accomplish the patient's individualized goals.

When it's used. Music therapy helps decrease physical pain, lower heart rate and blood pressure, reduce stress, improve sleep, boost memory and cognitive function, and treat cardiac complications, cancer, diabetes, and diabetes.

The psychological benefits of music therapy include:
- Lifting one's mood.
- Increasing joy and awe.
- Reducing anxiety.
- Alleviating depression.
- Regulating emotions (particularly difficult ones).
- Facilitating self-reflection.
- Assisting in the processing of trauma.

How it works. This approach involves listening to, reflecting upon, and creating music under the guidance of a trained music therapist.

What to expect. The sessions are often one-on-one. After an initial assessment, the therapist tailors techniques to fit a client's musical ability, interests, and specific needs.

What to look for in a music therapist. Start by looking for a board-certified music therapist. In the U.S., the certification process requires therapists to complete an undergraduate or master's degree in music therapy at an approved institution along with clinical training and a supervised internship. Therapists then must complete a board certification test. The Certification Board for Music Therapists grants practitioners the credential MT-BC (Music Therapist-Board Certified).

Narrative Therapy

Narrative counseling views people as separate from their problems and destructive behaviors. The core aspects include:

- The deconstruction of problematic and dominant storylines or narratives.

- Breaking the narrative into smaller and more manageable chunks.

- Rewriting the script of the problematic and dominant storylines.

- Broadening your view and moving toward healthier storylines (this is also called the *unique outcomes technique*, which may help us better understand our experiences and emotions).

- What is true for one person may not be true for all or another.

- Externalizing the problem because you are not the problem.

- A healthy narrative helps us make meaning and see purpose.

When it's used. Narrative therapy is used for individuals, couples, and families (specifically people who define themselves by their problems). Further, people who suffer from anxiety, depression, trauma, addictions, eating disorders, anger, and general difficulties with emotional regulation benefit from this type of therapy.

How it works. In narrative therapy, the events that occur over time in a person's life are viewed as stories, some of which stand out as more significant or fateful than others. These significant stories, usually stemming from negative events, can ultimately shape one's identity. Beyond this identity, the narrative therapist views a client's life as multitiered and full of possibilities just waiting to be discovered. The therapist does not act as an expert. Instead, he or she helps clients see how they are the experts regarding their own lives and how they can uncover the dreams, goals, and skills that define who they are (separate from their problems).

What to expect. A narrative therapist will direct the conversation by asking you what you prefer to talk about and, on an ongoing schedule, check in to see if the topic, which is most likely a problem, is still something you're interested in discussing. After a time, he or she may lead you to tell another more positive story from your life to help you discover inherent traits and skills.

What to look for in a narrative therapist. A narrative therapist is a licensed mental health professional, social worker, or therapist who has additional training in narrative therapy through academic programs, intensive workshops, or online continuing education.

There are even more types of therapy that you can discover online. However, when it comes to defragging your mind through therapy, make sure that you and your therapist understand and are aligned with your objectives and goals.

Chapter Eight

Get Your Sh** Together

"Our life is shaped by our mind, for we become what we think. Joy follows a pure thought like a shadow that never leaves."

–Buddha

Unfortunately, even with all the information you have received through this book, you are likely to have challenges and setbacks. But that's okay… as long as you learn from them and never stop striving for success.

Please also remember that because defragging your mind is both a conscious and subconscious activity, meditation and mindfulness are essential for every step of your journey.

If you still aren't convinced, here are the benefits of defragging your mind.

- **Increased cognitive function.** Our brains process a vast amount of information every day, and this mental activity can lead to fragmentation. Just like a fragmented hard drive slows down, a cluttered mind also impairs cognitive function. Mind defragmentation assists you in streamlining your thoughts, allowing you to think more clearly, make wiser decisions, and solve problems more efficiently.

- **Reduced stress and anxiety.** A fragmented mind is often associated with stress and anxiety because without organization, thoughts and worries pile up, and that leads to overwhelm. Through defragmentation, you can create a sense of order, reduce anxiety, and enhance your overall mental well-being.

- **Enhanced creativity.** A defragged mind is like a blank, open canvas for creativity. When your thoughts are organized, you can more easily tap into your creativity, and the clarity allows innovative ideas to flow freely.

- **Improved productivity.** A well-organized mind acts with efficiency and productivity. When your mind is decluttered, you can tackle tasks more effectively, and you'll find it easier to focus, set goals, and accomplish tasks without being sidetracked by fragmented thoughts.

In summary, here are six essential steps to take to defrag your mind.

- **Mindfulness meditation**. Regular mindfulness and meditation help you become more aware of your thoughts, emotions, and mental patterns. It can also help you make your thoughts and behavior patterns more positive.

- **Declutter your physical environment**. Your external environment often reflects your internal self. Having a clean and organized space will more than likely promote a clean and organized mind.

- **Prioritize and plan**. To defrag your mind, you need to set clear priorities. Creating to-do lists, establishing goals, and allocating specific time slots for tasks can help you accomplish this.

- **Practice mindful breathing**. When you feel overwhelmed, take a moment to pause and engage in the breathing exercise of your choice. It will help you regain the mental clarity you need.

- **Digital detox**. Our persistent connection and attention to devices can lead to information overload and fragmentation. Taking regular screen breaks helps you maintain a more focused mind.

- **Learn to say no**. Overcommitting to yourself and others can lead to mental clutter. Be selective with the tasks and plans you make.

Defragging your mind is a vital step toward achieving peak mental performance and overall well-being. By reducing mental clutter, improving cognitive function, and enhancing creativity, you will unlock your full potential and live your best life.

So, please—get out there and start to make sh** happen!

Your Action Plan

Taking notes as you work through this book will result in an inspiring collection of next steps to keep your motivation and momentum when you're done reading. Putting a date on your next action step and adding it to your calendar will strengthen your commitment to yourself.

Chapter 1: Find Your Focus

What mental focus techniques are you interested in trying? Note some resources you know about or find on the internet.

Technique I'm interested in trying	My next steps	Date I'll take my next steps
Meditation		
Hypnotherapy		
Yoga		
Music		
Breath Work		
Artwork		
Journaling		
Tai Chi		
Acupuncture		
EFT Tapping		
Technology cleanse		
Decluttering		
Other		

Chapter 2: Decide What You Want

What two things do I want most in my life?

What do I *know* rather than *hope*?

What do I have gratitude for, and how can I practice gratitude every day?

How do I prioritize tasks?

How do I prioritize my plans for how I do I spend time?

How do I identify and live my values?

Chapter 3: Ignore the Rest

Can you identify some of the baggage you carry that you'd like to offload?

Record your action steps for addressing them.

Technique I'm interested in trying	My next steps	Date I'll take my next steps
Self-reflection and journaling		
Meditation and/or hypnotherapy		
Support groups		

Educational workshops and seminars		
Physical activity		
Self-help books		
Life coaching or therapy		
Online resources and communities		
Creative expression		
Other		

Chapter 4: Cleaning Out the Recycle Bin

Emotive journaling is a proven method of working through some of the baggage you carry. Create an action plan for you to try it.

What do I need in order to try emotive journaling?

When will I do it? Create a schedule for your first month of journaling and put it on your calendar. Commit to caring for yourself and put it on your schedule just as you would a work or friend commitment.

Where will I do it? Identify a place that will support your success and make sure it's ready for you.

Why will I do it? Having a clear reason that you review regularly will keep you motivated. Write it here, in your journal, and anywhere else you'll see.

Chapter 5: Managing Habits

Habits that Destroy Creativity	**How I Indulge that Habit**	**What I'd Rather Do**
Assuming things will "just happen."		
Failing to support the creative process.		
Ignoring the opinions of others.		
Multitasking.		
Insisting on perfectionism.		
Getting stuck in the research phase.		
Letting yourself get stuck in a rut.		
Believing that social time doesn't take you away from your creative time.		

Worksheet for working on bad habits

The habit I want to work on: _____.

What triggers this habit?

How can I disrupt each of those triggers?

What positive new habit can I use to replace the bad habit? (These should be small, achievable steps.)

Why do I want to change this habit? What will be the result that makes it worth working on?

How do I motivate myself to keep going and turn my new positive behaviors into positive habits?

Chapter 6: Seeking Novelty

What are some ideas from Chapter 6 you'd like to implement to incorporate novelty into your life?

Here are the steps to identifying possible hobbies or activities you'd like to explore.

- Record some general life goals you have right now.

- Note some activities or skills that attract you. Dream big! Don't worry about practicality at this point; just write down things that perk your interest or you've always wanted to experience.

- Break down those attractions into what you actually desire. *Why* do you want to travel to Italy? What exactly would riding horses add to your life?

- Now list the substance or essence of what you want.

- What hobbies offer some of the substance of what you want and interface with the life goals you mentioned in the first step?

Record each idea, hobby, or activity you want to try and how you will do so.

Activities I'm interested in trying	My next steps	Date I'll take my next steps

Chapter 7: Manage Your Mood

What steps do you want to take to learn to manage your moods?

Mood-management Tool	My next steps	Date I'll take my next steps
Physical activity		
Rewards		
Diet and nutrition		
Social interaction		
Therapy		

Conclusion

Dear reader,

As we reach the end of our journey together through the pages of this book, it's time to reflect on the path you're about to embark on.

Imagine a life full of clarity, productivity, and happiness. All of that is possible for you when you do the work to defrag your mind.

However, as you stand on this threshold of change, please remember that it's a journey and not a destination. Growth, especially when it comes to defragging your mind, is a lifestyle that requires constant effort to face the daily events that jeopardize your mental clarity and health.

But where to start? Pick one activity—be it yoga, meditation, EFT tapping, etc.—and slowly experiment with others to find the combination best for you and your mind.

Moreover, don't be afraid to reach out to friends, family, an online community, etc., when you feel like you could use some help. Nobody is in this alone.

We hope this book has been a valuable guide. We hope that it has motivated and inspired you to make changes in your life.

Dear reader, as you turn to the final page of this book, remember that this isn't the end. Instead, it's just the beginning—the beginning of a new way of living and a new way of being—to a life without mental blockages and negative thoughts.

Thank you for joining us on this journey, and thank you for choosing to make a change.

With heartfelt gratitude and best wishes for your continued journey,

Deborah LeBlanc

Additional Resources

Books

Anxiety: The Missing Stage of Grief: A Revolutionary Approach to Understanding and Healing the Impact of Loss, by Claire Bidwell Smith, LCPC (2020)

- From the Amazon description: "If you're suffering from anxiety but not sure why, or if you're struggling with loss and looking for solace, *Anxiety: The Missing Stage of Grief* offers help and answers. As grief expert Claire Bidwell Smith discovered in her own life—and in her practice with her therapy clients—significant loss and unresolved grief are primary underpinnings of anxiety. Using research and real-life stories, Smith breaks down the physiology of anxiety, providing a concrete explanation that will help you heal. Starting with the basics questions—"What is anxiety?" and "What is grief?" and moving to concrete approaches such as making amends, taking charge, and retraining your brain, *Anxiety* takes a big step beyond Elisabeth Kübler-Ross›s widely accepted five stages to unpack everything from our age-old fears about mortality to the bare vulnerability a loss can make us feel."

Cognitive Behavioral Therapy & Mindfulness (2 books in 1), by Olivia Telford (2021).

- From the Amazon description: "Cognitive Behavioral Therapy (CBT) and Mindfulness go hand in hand in improving your wellbeing and offer new ways to strengthen your emotional state. It's so easy to let your mind slip destructively and allow it to run from thought to thought and worry to worry. It's time to challenge and educate yourself with approaches that work. CBT and Mindfulness are quickly becoming the most popular tools in the field of psychology. In *Cognitive Behavioral Therapy and Mindfulness: 2 Books in 1*, you will dive into what it takes to process your thoughts through CBT. You will find eye-opening strategies and exercises to lead you to a healthier and stronger sense of self."

Control Your Mind and Master Your Feelings, by Eric Robertson (2019)

- From the Amazon description: "We oftentimes look towards the outside world to find the roots of our problems. However, most of the time, we should be looking inward. Our mind and our emotions determine our state of being in the present moment. If those aspects are left unchecked, we can get easily overwhelmed and are left feeling unfulfilled every single day."

Deep Clearing: Balance Your Emotions, Let Go of Inner & Outer Negativity, Shift to Higher Consciousness: A Radical Inner Process, by John Ruskan (2021)

- From the Amazon description: "Drawing upon his 25 years as a holistic psychotherapist, John Ruskan presents a brilliant self-therapy system for complete inner healing and well-being. Based on a unique synthesis of Eastern meditation-mindfulness principles and Western humanistic psychological insights, the **DEEP CLEARING** program will empower you with a feeling-based, holistic, inner process that will clear the subconscious, restore and maintain emotional balance, overcome inner and outer negativity, and spontaneously shift you into authentic unconditional joyfulness and Higher Consciousness."

Don't Believe Everything You Think, by Joseph Nguyen (2022)

- From the Amazon description: "Learn how to overcome anxiety, self-doubt & self-sabotage without needing to rely on motivation or willpower."

EFT Tapping: Quick and Simple Exercises to De-Stress, Re-Energize, and Overcome Emotional Problems Using Emotional Freedom Technique, by Mike Moreland (2014).

- From the Amazon description: "Do you feel stressed out a lot of the time? Do you often feel tired and worn out? Is your mind occupied with problems and do you struggle with emotional issues? You're not alone! These are common issues that a lot of people face today. Fortunately, there are plenty of good methods that can be used to resolve these kinds of issues. There's cognitive therapy, talk therapy, meditation, yoga, etc. These methods can definitely be helpful. However, they are not always as easy to learn and seeing a therapist can get pretty expensive. This book deals with a different technique that may work better for you: EFT Tapping. It is effective, easy to learn and quick to do: you can already feel better after just a few minutes! Also, EFT is a simple self-help technique, so you don't need an expensive therapist. In this book, you will learn how to do a standard EFT Tapping session to work on any issue you may have."

Help Me Stop Overthinking: The Ultimate Guide to Stop Overthinking and Live Your Best Life, by Vaughn Carter (2023)

- From the Amazon description: "Whether you're fixating on how much to tip, overanalyzing a text message, or imagining the worst-case scenario, overthinking is a stressful waste of time. When overthinking is your constant companion, it can feel impossible to take action or focus on anything. As a result, your career, your relationships, and your well-being all suffer – overtaken by your regrets, fears, and anxieties. But your thoughts don't have to control your life. You can take back control of your mind, stop overthinking, and actually appreciate and enjoy life. With the guidance of this book, you'll be able to cultivate a more mindful approach, gain more clarity, and navigate uncertainty with confidence."

I'm Working On It in Therapy: How to Get the Most Out of Psychotherapy, by Gary Trosclair (2015)

- From the Amazon description: "Millions of Americans will go to therapy this year, but veteran psychotherapist Gary Trosclair believes the vast majority of them will start the process with little to no sense of how to best use their sessions to achieve their goals. Recent research has identified effective client participation as one of the most crucial factors in successful therapy. What can one do to get the most out of their sessions to create lasting positive changes in their lives? What does it look like to "work on it" in therapy? Trosclair covers these points and more, combining cutting-edge scientific research with years of fascinating anecdotal evidence to create a guide that is as compelling as it is indispensable."

Make Sh** Happen! How to Unleash REAL Power Into Your Life, by Deborah LeBlanc (2024)

- Deborah LeBlanc's *Make Sh** Happen* is a call to action for dreamers stuck in neutral. Consider this book the first stepping stone on your pathway toward true accomplishment. Inside, you'll discover a treasure trove of wisdom, from myth-busting science to productivity hacks that make progress feel like playtime. You'll map your trajectory by way of insightful exercises, then watch your efficiency soar—at last. With witty warmth and cold hard facts, this little book will make a big difference, facilitating a mindset shift that's guaranteed to take you off the sofa and test your limits. The outcome? A life you've only imagined—a life you've never dared to claim. It's time to cut through the nasty habits, endless excuses, and sloppy plans. It's time to work smart instead of hard. It's time to make sh** happen!

Make Sh** Happen! Improve Your Memory, by Deborah LeBlanc (2024)

- Deborah LeBlanc's latest installment of the acclaimed Make Sh** Happen series is a humor-laden, practical guide to boosting your memory fast. Skillfully blending comedic flair with astounding data-driven advice, LeBlanc tackles everything from forgetfulness to cognitive health with her characteristic wit and warmth.

Make Sh** Happen! Unclutter Your Life, by Deborah LeBlanc (2024)

- This volume of Deborah LeBlanc's Make Sh** Happen Series is a wry yet insightful guide to cleaning your closet...and very existence. It isn't time to just tidy up. It's time to completely transform—together. From physical mounds and digital masses to crippling mental sloppiness, Deborah has tactics proven to help break free of all disorder.

Mindful Moments: Mindfulness Strategies for Women in the Modern World, by Sophia Bennet (2024)

- From the Amazon description: "Welcome to a transformative exploration of mindfulness and self-compassion designed to usher you into serenity, understanding, and growth. "Mindful Moments" is crafted to guide you on a journey of self-discovery and emotional resilience. This book, composed of two distinct yet interconnected parts, invites women to delve into practices that enhance mindfulness and foster a compassionate relationship with themselves amidst the complexities of modern life."

Mind Shift: It Doesn't Take a Genius to Think Like One, by Erwin Raphael McManus (2023)

- From the Amazon description: "Mental toughness, mental clarity, and mental health all have one thing in common: The journey begins in your mind. In this radical guide, the award-winning author of *The Last Arrow* illuminates a surprising path toward personal fulfillment and optimal performance."

On Grief and Grieving: Finding the Meaning of Grief Through Five Stages of Loss, by Elisabeth Kübler-Ross, David Kessler, et al. (2014)

- From the Amazon description: "A modern classic text on the crucial role of grieving in dealing with loss, by the author who first explored the now-famous five stages of grief—*On Grief and Grieving* is an invaluable blend of Kubler-Ross's practical wisdom, case studies, and her own experiences and spiritual insight."

Practicing Mindfulness: 75 Essential Meditations to Reduce Stress, Improve Mental Health, and Find Peace in the Everyday, by Matthew Sockolov (2018)

- From the Amazon description: "Mindfulness is an evidence-based method for reducing stress and anxiety, enhancing resilience, and maintaining mental well-being. Even short meditations can turn a bad day around, ground us in the present moment, and help us approach life with gratitude and kindness. This mindfulness book was created by the founder of One Mind Dharma. He developed these 75 essential exercises to offer practical guidance for anyone who wants to realize the benefits of being more mindful."

Practical Optimism: The Art, Science, and Practice of Exceptional Well-Being, by Sue Varma, MD (2024)

- From the Amazon description: "A practical program rooted in optimism to help you live fully and joyfully in an imperfect, turbulent world."

Simple Serenity: Five-Minute Meditations for Everyday Life, by Josie Robinson (2022)

- From the Amazon description: "In difficult and stressful times, peace can be hard to come by. That's why you need a quick solution to help you find calm and serenity—no matter what the world throws your way. Using the simple guided meditations inside this beautiful little book, you'll learn how to slow down, relax, and appreciate what's good in your life—all in just five minutes a day."

Stop Overthinking: 23 Techniques to Relieve Stress, Stop Negative Spirals, Declutter Your Mind, and Focus on the Present, by Nick Trenton (2021)

- -From the Amazon description: Overcome negative thought patterns, reduce stress, and live a worry-free life. Overthinking is the biggest cause of unhappiness. Don›t get stuck in a never-ending thought loop. Stay present and keep your mind off things that don›t matter, and never will. Break free of your self-imposed mental prison. Stop Overthinking is a book that understands what you've been through, the exhausting situation you've put yourself into, and how you lose your mind in the trap of anxiety and stress. Acclaimed author Nick Trenton will walk you through the obstacles with detailed and proven techniques to help you rewire your brain, control your thoughts, and change your mental habits. What's more, the book will provide you with scientific approaches to completely change the way you think and feel about yourself by ending the vicious thought patterns.

Switch In Your Brain: The Key to Peak Happiness, Thinking, and Health, by Caroline Leaf (2013)

- From the Amazon description: "Supported by current scientific and medical research, Dr. Caroline Leaf gives readers a prescription for better health and wholeness through correct thinking patterns, declaring that we are not victims of our biology. She shares with readers the "switch" in our brains that enables us to live happier, healthier, more enjoyable lives where we achieve our goals, maintain our weight, and even become more intelligent. She shows us how to choose life, get our minds under control, and reap the benefits of a detoxed thought life."

The Art of Letting Go: How to Let Go of the Past, Look Forward to the Future, and Finally Enjoy the Emotional Freedom You Deserve, by Damon Zahariades (2022)

- From the Amazon description: "Finally Let Go of Your Negative Thoughts and Enjoy the Emotional Freedom You Deserve! Are you struggling with anger, regrets, and resentment? Do you feel emotionally exhausted, stressed, and discouraged by painful memories? Are you holding on to things that are making you feel miserable? If so, THE ART OF LETTING GO is for you."

The Gratitude Jar: A Simple Guide to Creating Miracles, by Josie Robinson (2014)

- From the Amazon description: "*The Gratitude Jar* is a book that has come to light when the world deeply needs to read its message. The story itself is a heartwarming, inspirational tale of spiritual transformation and self-discovery, but it is also a guidebook with the power to instantly release the negative belief systems no longer serving you....and to direct your steps with new energy onto the path of joy and personal freedom."

The Little Book of Mindfulness: 10 Minutes a Day to Less Stress, More Peace, by Dr. Patrizia Collard (2014)

- From the Amazon description: "*The Little Book of Mindfulness* is a beautifully color-illustrated book of 40 easy ways to be mindful every day. Mindfulness is the easy way to gently let go of stress and be in the moment. It has fast become the slow way to manage the modern world—without chanting mantras or finding hours of special time to meditate. Dr. Patrizia Collard will show you how to bring simple 5- and 10-minute practices into your day in order to free yourself from stress and, ultimately, find more peace in your life."

The Power of Awareness: Unlocking the Law of Attraction, by Neville Goddard (1952)

From the Amazon description: "Venturing into the realms of mysticism and religion, Neville's work is rooted in an empowering insistence on the agency of individuals to shape their own reality."

The Power of Your Subconscious Mind, by Dr. Joseph Murphy (2020)

- From the Amazon description: "Did you know that your mind has a 'mind' of its own? Yes! Without even realizing it, our mind is often governed by another entity which is called the sub-conscious mind. In this book, the author fuses his spiritual wisdom and scientific research to bring to light how the subconscious mind can be a major influence on our daily lives. Once you understand your subconscious mind, you can also control or get rid of the various phobias that you may have in turn opening a brand-new world of positive energy."

The Soul Happy Book: Reprogram Your Mind Using Groundbreaking Techniques Bridging Science and Spirituality, by Tracy Zboril, MSW, and Cara Hewett, MA (2018)

- From the Amazon description: "Seasoned therapists, Tracy Zboril, M.S.W., and Cara Hewett, M.A. present their groundbreaking work, *The Soul Happy Book* written to help you reprogram your mind. Exhausted and disheartened by decades of working with patients in private therapy practices and seeing little to no results, Zboril and Hewett threw in the towel on traditional talk therapy. Diving head first into research on alternative psychotherapy techniques, neuroscience, and the ancient wisdom of spirituality, they discovered that traditional talk therapy is so ineffective because it works with the wrong part of the brain."

The Tapping Solution: A Revolutionary System for Stress-Free Living, by Nick Ortner (2013).

From the Amazon Description: "In the *New York Times* best-selling book *The Tapping Solution*, Nick Ortner, founder of the Tapping World Summit and best-selling filmmaker of The Tapping Solution, is at the forefront of a new healing movement. In this book, he gives readers everything they need to successfully start using the powerful practice of tapping—or Emotional Freedom Techniques (EFT). Tapping is one of the fastest and easiest ways to address both the emotional and physical problems that tend to hamper our lives."

Things That Matter: Overcoming Distraction to Pursue a More Meaningful Life, by Joshua Becker (2022)

From the Amazon description: "In *Things That Matter,* Joshua Becker uses practical exercises, questions, insights from a nationwide survey, and success stories to give you the motivation you need to: identify pursuits that matter most to you, align your dreams with your daily priorities, recognize how money and possessions keep you from happiness, become aware of how others' opinions of you influence your choices, embrace what you're truly passionate about instead of planning that next escape, figure out what to do with all those emails, notifications, and pings, and let go of past mistakes and debilitating habits."

Think Again, by Adam Grant (2023)

- From the Amazon description: "The #1 *New York Times* bestselling author of *Give and Take* and *Originals* examines the critical art of rethinking: learning to question your opinions and open other people›s minds, which can position you for excellence at work and wisdom in life."

Today I Noticed: A Little Book of Mindfulness That Will Change the Way You See The World, by Willow Older and Deborah Huber (2023)

- From the Amazon description: "Slow down and appreciate the little moments in daily life with this inspirational mindfulness book from the team behind Today I Noticed. How often do you stop to notice the small moments in every ordinary day? With its simple, three-word prompt and heartwarming illustrations, *Today I Noticed* celebrates the power of slowing down and noticing the world around us. A beautiful gift book for anyone seeking to build a simple and fun daily mindfulness practice, *Today I Noticed* features artwork and musings that will inspire you to express gratitude for the little moments that often slip by unnoticed."

Websites

FreeMindfulness.org

- Get free downloadable mindfulness meditation exercises.

Mindful.org

- Find blog posts, guided meditations, and podcasts about having and maintaining a healthy mind and a healthy life.

MindPathTherapies.com

- The author of the *Make Sh** Happen* series' website. It provides resources on what hypnosis is and is not, various information on workshops she is offering, guided hypnotherapy audios, the opportunity to book her for one-on-one sessions, and more!

- Hypnotherapies can be purchased to address the following topics:
  - Anxiety Release
  - Assertiveness
  - Brain Power
  - Creativity
  - Deep Relaxation
  - Exercise Motivation
  - Guilt Release
  - Increase Self-Esteem
  - Insecurity
  - Motivation
  - Overcoming Shame
  - Performance Anxiety
  - Powerful Public Speaking
  - Problem-Solving
  - Stress Release
  - Worrying

TheTappingSolution.com

- As featured on *CNN, Psychology Today, Women's Health, and Cosmopolitan,* this site gives you all the information you could want on the exercise of tapping.

ZenHabits.net

- A website about "finding the simplicity and mindfulness in the daily chaos of our lives," led by Leo Babauta, a father, author, and simplicity coach.

Podcasts featuring Deborah LeBlanc

Buision – "Writing and Selling Books in Today's Age (With Deborah LeBlanc)." (Season 1, Episode 2)

Happily Ever Habits (January 25, 2022)

I Never Knew (INK) But My Dog Did! with Life coach Maureen – "Loss, Love, and

Paranormal Entities." (Episode 32)

Life's Multiverse – "Rising from the Ashes with Deborah LeBlanc: On Resilience and Self-Limiting Beliefs." (December 8, 2023)

Resilient Minds 365 – "Deborah LeBlanc, Clinical Depression and Hypnotherapy." (Episode 57)

The Day After with CJ & Ashley – "Bringing Color Back into the World w/ Deborah LeBlanc." (Episode 17)

The Flare Up Show – "Letting Go of Limiting Beliefs." (Episode 62)

The Story Behind the Story with Matteo and Renata (Episode 60).

Trauma Unbroken Podcast with Michael Unbroken – "How to Find Yourself with Deborah LeBlanc." (Episode 249)

Other Podcasts

10% Happier with Dan Harris

- Dan Harris is a journalist who experienced the benefits of mindfulness and meditation in treating his anxiety.

Mindfulness Mode

- An interview-based podcast about the scientific and practical aspects of mindfulness.

On Being

- Hosted by Krista Tippett and created as a digital gathering place for anyone interested in mindfulness.

Untangle: Mindfulness for Curious Humans

- Hosted by former social media executives who are known for developing a headband that helps improve the quality of meditation sessions.

About the Author

Deborah LeBlanc is a Certified Clinical Hypnotherapist with certifications in ten other healing modalities that span seventy presenting issues. Her expertise in relationship building has afforded her the opportunity to travel throughout the country as a keynote speaker and workshop facilitator.

www.ingramcontent.com/pod-product-compliance
Lightning Source LLC
Chambersburg PA
CBHW070107080526
44586CB00013B/1217